CHINA BUSINESS CULTURE

Strategies for Success

CHINA BUSINESS CULTURE

Strategies for Success

Yuan Wang
Xin Sheng Zhang
Rob Goodfellow

THOROGOOD

Text Copyright © Yuan Wang, Xin Sheng Zhang, Rob Goodfellow, 2003
Layout and Design © Talisman Publishing Pte Ltd

First published in 2003
Reprinted @ 2005 (Text Correction)

Southeast Asia
Talisman Publishing Pte Ltd
52, Genting Lane #06-05
Ruby Land Complex Block 1
Singapore 349560

Rest of the World
Thorogood
10-12 Rivington Street
London EC2A 3DU
Phone: 020 7749 4748
Fax: 020 7729 6110
E-mail: info@thorogood.ws

ISBN 981-04-9158-1

Printed in Malaysia by Percetakan Warisan Sdn Bhd

Foreword

In the last quarter of the 20th century the key regions in China created one of the strongest and most dynamic marketing economies in the world, with its own distinctively 'Chinese flavour'. This emerging model of commerce should ensure future growth and prosperity for China well into the 21st Century. China will continue to provide international business with many exciting and profitable commercial opportunities as the effective demand of its potential market of 1. 3 billion people slowly develops an enhanced communications infrastructure. How to successfully enter the Chinese market is the preoccupation of foreign businesses presently interested in China, particularly with China's entry to The World Trade Organisation (WTO) and the announcement that Beijing will host the 2008 Olympic Games.

In *China Business Culture: Strategies for Success* some of these important questions concerning the character of the Chinese market are addressed in a timely and comprehensive fashion. Significantly, all three authors, Dr Yuan Wang, Associate Professor Xin-Sheng Zhang, and Dr Rob Goodfellow have been exposed to both 'Western' and 'Eastern' cultures. In this sense they are 'culturally bilingual'. As a crystallisation of the authors' experiences and research, this book constitutes an important contribution to cross-cultural understanding. It provides readers with deep insights into Chinese business culture. It will be a valuable tool for those Western businesspeople or managers who wish to enter and succeed in the Chinese market, as well as students of business and commerce at both undergraduate and post-graduate MBA level.

It is with great pleasure that I commend this book as an

important contribution to the development of a rapidly maturing relationship between China and the international business community. China is undergoing major and sometimes extraordinary changes in its economic and social structures, as are many of her major trading partners. This change has pushed forward unprecedented change in practically every field of human endeavour – including international commerce. The realities of constant change at the dawn of the new 'era of globalisation' means that previously held views about what constitutes a distinctive business culture must be constantly re-examined. Business culture in China is no different. The authors have presented a vivid and very current picture of modern-day commerce in the People's Republic of China.

China Business Culture: Strategies for Success illustrates creatively a number of key areas of interest seldom combined in one book. These areas include, a discussion of Chinese managerial style, the significance of business networks, the best way to co-operate with various departments of the Chinese government, skills of negotiation, the cultural 'essence' of Chinese commerce, Chinese consumer psychology and the most effective way of promoting goods and services in the 'world's largest market'.

Stewart R. Clegg,
Professor of Management UTS
PO Box 123
Broadway NSW 2007
Australia

Contents

Personnel - *Recruiting the Right people*
Protection - *Legal Security*
Perspective - *Cultural Sensitivity*

Preface

China is undergoing major and indeed extraordinary changes in its economic and social structures. This change has resulted in unprecedented convergence in practically every field of endeavour – including international trade and commerce.

The realities of constant change at the dawn of the 'era of globalisation' means that stereotypical or traditional views about what constitutes a distinctive business culture must be constantly re-examined. In this book we have presented a vivid picture of modern-day commerce in the People's Republic of China, written in a practical, comprehensive style, that will appeal to a wide spectrum of readers – from professional businesspeople and MBA postgraduates, to university and business college students, and even high school seniors in dedicated Asian studies courses.

This book is written to meet the growing demand for new knowledge about the world's largest market, particularly in light China's entry into WTO and the opportunities associated with preparations for the 2008 Beijing Olympic Games. We believe that our material will easily keep the interest of anyone wishing to better understand China's rich history and corporate culture.

China Business Culture: Strategies for Success does not attempt to explain China's complex business environment in terms of tradition alone, but also looks at commerce as a dynamic expression of a living, changing culture. Our challenge has been to provide a wide readership with new tools to understand the transforming process of change.

Each chapter features a convenient, concise and 'reader friendly' introduction, with individual case-studies used to illustrate major themes. Material is then structured in layers, each providing a foundation for the chapter to follow. For example, China's international trade history and commercial development is explained in the context of Confucianism and traditional Chinese business values. This demonstrates that modern Chinese business values are evidence of a revolution in commerce. In turn, this point is expanded by explaining the complex but predictable rules of the Chinese negotiating 'game' – new skills that must be learned, practised and applied.

General characteristics of Chinese business culture are explained in detail. The book also prepares the reader for current information on co-ordinating activities within complicated business networks. In the chapters to follow readers will learn how to enter into exciting speciality fields by effective marketing, and by the application of Chinese customer psychology.

China Business Culture: Strategies for Success concludes all of its aspects by a discussion of the six 'P's of successful business in China: 'Patience', 'Power' in finance, 'Predisposition' in policies and relationships, 'Personnel', 'Protection' with legal security, and the 'Perspective' of cultural sensitivity.

Throughout the writing of the book the authors have used the terms "foreign" and "westerner" interchangeably.

Finally we would like to acknowledge the assistance and support of numerous associates including Professor Stewart R. Clegg, School of Management, the University of Technology Sydney, Professor John Glynn, Dean of Economics, the University of Wollongong/Sydney Business School, Mr Fan-Sheng Gou, Chairman, Huiecong International Group, Mr Clarence Da Gama Pinto, Program Director, Mt Eliza Business School, Mr Martin O'Shannessy, Executive Director, IRIS Research and Mr Jonar C. Nader, Chairman of consulting firm Logictivity Pty Ltd.

We would like to thank both Mr Zhao Ji Ping and Ms Ji-Nong Wang, for professional assistance with current Chinese market data.

The responsibility for opinions and judgements expressed in this book however are purely those of the authors.

Introduction

In the past three decades China has experienced four historical events of international significance. The first was the restoration of China's legal status as a sovereign nation by the Security Council of the United Nations in 1970. The second was the 'Open Door' policy of 1978. The third has been China's winning bid for the 2008 Olympics. The fourth was China's successful entry into the World Trade Organisation (WTO) in late 2001.

The decision of the International Olympic Committee (IOC) to award Beijing the 2008 Summer Games presents two opportunities. According to World Bank estimates, the People's Republic of China (PRC) intends to spend more than $US20 billion over the next seven years on infrastructure modernisation alone. This commitment will ensure that the event is not only a sporting success, but will also mark China's emergence as an outward looking, and fully integrated member of the international community.

The second opportunity is that while China opened her doors to the world in 1978, she is now about to open all the windows as well. The IOC decision means that China is currently attracting an unprecedented level of attention from the international community. This will expose China to a second 'great opening movement'; where reform of economic infrastructure and new social development programmes continue to drive investment. China attracts more foreign direct investment (FDI) today than any country except for the USA. Over twenty years of sustained reform has seen China emerge as one of the major players in the world economy.

China's transformation from a centralised, Soviet-style planned economy to a market economy has invigorated China's capacity to do business. A research report released by the investment bank, Goldman Sachs, in July 2001 and confirmed by the World Bank, predicts that China's GDP will grow by 7 per cent each year for the next seven years. This means that China has been able to maintain an average growth rate of 8 per cent for the past 30 years. This is unprecedented in the economic history of the world.

China's own interests now lie in gaining access to every imaginable field of knowledge and expertise. This is because the Olympics are all about China presenting her best face to the world. To strengthen China's reputation as a modern, outwardly-looking nation, the Chinese Government has indicated that in addition to developing the Beijing-based Olympic site, there will also be a more general programme of urban renewal, which will include housing, communications infrastructure technology, mass transport systems and environment protection schemes that will reduce pollution and stabilise land degradation. (China ratified the Kyoto protocol in late 2002 paving the way for the importation of a very broad range of environmental technologies to meet the PRC's ambitious program). It must be said, though, that the Olympics did not start this process. On the contrary, nowhere can China's transformation be seen more clearly than in Beijing's fifteen-year preparation for admittance to the WTO, ratified in Doha, Qatar, in November 2001.

Entry to WTO will bring to fruition two decades of economic transition to a unique type of free market economy, regulating China's position as 'the workshop of the world' and freeing up China's financial, insurance and banking sectors. In time this will provide enormous new opportunities for foreign investors.

China is not a newcomer to international trade. The Chinese believe that the 'Great Dragon' ruled the Middle Kingdom of the world for nearly four thousand years. For most of this period, China was the greatest trading nation on Earth. Together with the Roman Empire, China was the superpower of antiquity. The Dragon then 'fell asleep' for two centuries while China collapsed under the co-opting and corrosive effects of colonialism. In 1978, the late Paramount Leader, Deng Xiao Ping woke the Dragon up again with the successful implementation of China's Open Door Policy. As the world now knows, China's successful Olympic Games bid and admittance to the WTO has heralded a new era. The Dragon is back and becoming stronger than ever. The Chinese Motherland is poised to again take her place as an economic and cultural superpower.

China still has much to do in order to achieve her full potential. China needs expertise, especially in the fields of good corporate governance, legal reform, business systems, financial analysis, accountancy, banking programmes, risk management and cross-cultural communication. The need for China to continue to modernise was highlighted in 'The Opacity Index – Corruption Perception Survey', published by the Price Waterhouse Coopers Endowment for the Study of Transparency and Sustainability, in June 2001. This report examined the legal structure, accounting standards and business regulations of thirty-five countries. Although Indonesia and Russia were identified as being more corrupt, China was the worst performer in the survey in terms of the opacity of its legal and regulatory structures. Many people believe that the Olympics of 2008 present China with an achievable goal to modernise every aspect of her business practices, and in particular the three most important conditions necessary to attract continued foreign investment, namely, the rule of law, bureaucratic transparency, and policy predictability.

These issues are not only essential requirements for international investment, trade and commerce, but they are also the concern of China's rapidly emerging middle classes, who have enthusiastically substituted the 'iron rice bowl' of cradle-to-grave socialism with a free market system. This group, representing some 130 million people or 10 per cent of China's population of 1.3 billion citizens (China has an urban population of nearly 450 million), are looking for a formalised system of jurisprudence to protect their social and economic interests. This strategic change, with its shift in emphasis from social equality to economic efficiency, is a powerful motor for China's modernisation programme and globalisation drive. At the same time it will guarantee a more prosperous and peaceful China.

Early evidence of this happening is that in late 2001 the Chinese Government initiated a crackdown on all levels of corruption, led by an investigation into securities-traders who were suspected of price manipulation practices. Further evidence of fundamental reform can also be seen in the decision of the China Communist Party (CCP) to reverse decades of history by allowing private businesspeople to join the 64.5 million-strong CCP. Significantly this was proclaimed just one week before the announcement of the decision of the International Olympic Committee to award China the 2008 Olympics in July 2001. This sent a positive signal to the world that China was open for business and enthusiastic to reform and modernise every sector of her economy. Leading Party cadres, who now include businesspeople, are expected to act as good corporate role models and to exert a positive influence on Chinese society. The new policy obviously intends that these businesspeople will continue to be at the vanguard of not only economic but also social change.

Clearly the Chinese Government has become very skilled at managing its own agenda. This not only includes the Olympics and WTO negations, but also the Most Favoured Nation Status (MFN) debate and the slow, delicate, but positive behind-the-scenes negotiations over the future re-integration of Taiwan into the People's Republic of China. In effect a common market between Taiwan and the Mainland already exists. This has established strong lines of communication, as well as mutual interests and a sense that both parties have much to gain from continued dialogue as a prelude to future political and economic integration. These strong economic ties will eventually form a solid base for national reunion, which is both supported and expected by 99.5 per cent of the Chinese population.

These developments present international businesses with an unprecedented opportunity to expand their business interests and in doing so contribute to the further commercial and social development of China. Undoubtedly, however, China remains a great mystery to most foreign business people, just as 'the West' is for most Chinese. In many respects, these two societies are really discrete worlds, or parallel civilisations, which before the colonial period developed in almost complete isolation from one another. When these worlds did meet, it was through the one-sided experience of European colonisation. It is not surprising that mutual misunderstanding between actual or potential business partners and investors often occur, despite the continued integration of the world economy and the globalisation of business practices. Unfortunately, the view of the West towards China continues to be coloured by the Tiananmen Square incident of 1989, while China's perception of the West is informed by the foreign incursions of over a century ago. Continued mistrust and feelings of risk in business between the West and China are illustrated by the fact that FDI in China by U.S and other Western-based multinational corporations (MNCs) has been surprisingly small. Less than one third of the total amount of in-bound FDI in China has come from the West, although China is the second largest recipient of FDI in the world.

To overcome these barriers, a proper understanding of the fundamental issue of cultural acclimatisation is a prerequisite. This must be mastered before businesspeople can begin to feel confident with more complex commercial interests. Understanding changing business values and the characteristics of Chinese business culture is a challenging project. Many Westerners succeed brilliantly in their efforts to do so. It is a process of accepting differences, adapting to change and adopting new way of managing across cultures. Unfortunately for every one cross-culturally-based commercially viable project that proceeds to the formal stage of business-to-business negotiations, it is estimated that up to nine out of ten fail because of 'misunderstandings'. Cultural risk factors have been not taken seriously enough by many businesspeople. This book addressees some common 'misunder-standings' based on cultural differences and provides useful remedies.

China is now in the middle of a second 'revolution' and recent changes have been so dramatic that most people in China have found it difficult to adapt. Foreign business people must be wary of accepting 'information' about China in preparation for the real world of commerce. Cultural information should be seen as the raw material of genuine understanding, which is a fluid process. Information is not necessarily 'understanding'. Data, like technology, can quickly become obsolete or irrelevant. Anyone who wants to enter the Chinese market, or just wants to know more about China's dynamic present must learn to craft their own unique approach. These lessons can then be applied to fresh challenges in an ever-changing situation.

This book concentrates on how best to operate in the China in spite of change. This business-like approach is based on certain core values, which partially transcend the inevitable turmoil of modernisation. This is the way that the Chinese themselves cope with modern life.

The 'Chinese way' is the subject of subsequent chapters, which will provide readers with a practical and comprehensive understanding of both the strategies and the skills required for doing business and keeping ahead of change in China. The book will answer a number of key questions. These include: What features characterise 'traditional' Chinese business culture? How has this changed? In what way does Chinese managerial style differ from that of the West? How do you effectively establish joint ventures? How do you best cooperate with various governmental departments? What is the most effective way of negotiating with Chinese businesspeople? What is the essence of the Chinese market? How do you explain consumer psychology? How do you use the custom of gift giving to increase your interpersonal and professional effectiveness? How does one conduct oneself at a formal banquet?

How should you effectively promote your products and services in China? And how do you overcome institutionalised corruption?

The answers to these questions are particularly relevant to multinational enterprises and global corporations who want to find their way into the Chinese market and in time to capitalise on the WTO 'gold rush'. Contemporary China's remarkable level of economic activity and robust demand for a vast range of goods and services makes these questions, and the Chinese market itself, impossible to ignore.

Chapter 1

China's International Trade History

This chapter summarizes China's history of international trade. For most of its long history China was a great trading power. However, from the colonial period until the late 1970s, China's history was not typified by forceful sovereignty, but by foreign invasion, civil war, and economic blockade, backed up by the military and technological superiority of the West. From 1978, the Chinese nation began to rediscover its former glory. It opened channels to international trade, welcomed foreign technological expertise, and began to create the social and ideological environment that would nurture the development of a modern market economy. The result is that in twenty years China has undergone a complete transformation from a sleeping, introvert giant, into a dynamic and modernising economic superpower. Indeed the Organisation for Economically Developed Countries (OECD) predicts that by 2015 China will surpass even the United States as the world's largest purchaser of goods and services. Important terms such as 'closed door' mentality, 'Self-Strengthening Movement', the 'Open Door' policy, and 'Mind Liberalisation' illustrate how China has achieved such a dramatic turn around. Together with nationalism, these concepts define what motivates the current Chinese leadership and explain the nation's desire for self-respect, self-sufficiency and prosperity.

Since 1978, China has consistently pursued what has been termed an 'Open Door' policy to international trade and investment. Implementation of the late Deng Xiao Ping's discrete programme of economic reform has clearly brought about remarkable changes in the economy, politics, social structure and culture of the PRC. The pace of these reforms has greatly impressed China's trading partners and it has amazed the Chinese people themselves. However, it is necessary to realise that China's experience of international trade did not start with the reforms of 1978, but dates back to a much earlier time.

China is an ancient civilisation with homogeneity of culture that spans from about 2500 B.C. to the present day. During this vast stretch of time, China has experienced glory, humiliation and nothing short of a miracle in her recent economic transformation and current standing in the world of international trade.

The Silk Road and Ocean Adventures

As early as the second century B.C., Han Dynasty traders established commercial links across half the globe. From this time, until the early nineteenth century, China was indisputably a great trading nation.

The first and most dynamic period of Chinese commercial expansion occurred during the Tang Dynasty (A.D. 618-907). At this time merchants traded goods internationally along a route which become known as the 'Silk Road'. The Silk Road began in Chang-An (Xi An city, the provincial capital of the present-day province of Shan Xi, and the capital of China during the Tang Dynasty). The route snaked westward, exiting China near Ka-shi, in the present-day province of Xin-Jiang, continuing on through Yamen, Northern India, Afghanistan and Persia, before finally ending in the Lebanese city-port of Tyre. From Tyre, goods were traded across the length and breath of Europe. During this prosperous era, Chinese, Middle Eastern and European merchants, adventurers, missionaries and officials all travelled along the Silk Road, trading with each other as they went. The commodities they exchanged included silk, spices, tea and ceramics.

China's next period of rapid expansion occurred during the Ming Dynasty. Between 1405 and 1433, Chinese merchants conducted seven commercial voyages to the ports of Southeast Asia and East Africa with the specific purpose of expanding Imperial China's trading power and influence. The first of these expeditionary voyages, under the great Admiral Zheng He involved sixty-two ships and 27,870 men, including representatives of the Imperial Court, clerks, accountants and buyers. These journeys brought great wealth and prestige to China and clearly demonstrated China's capacity to trade internationally.

The pre-eminence of China in the arts, culture, and trade during medieval times not only had a significant influence on its immediate neighbours, but also attracted European interest. In the early sixteenth century, European-trading vessels began to arrive off the shores of Mainland China. In 1557 Portuguese merchants were given permission to establish a commercial base in Macao. Thereafter a trade war ensued, with British and Dutch companies seizing every opportunity to challenge Portuguese pre-eminence. It was during this period — the late Ming and early Qing Dynasty — that China first attempted to limit the influence of the outside world.

The eighteenth and nineteenth centuries saw a contest between China's diminishing influence as a trading power and the growing influence of Europe. The 'closed door' mentality first took place in China at a time when the West was rapidly industrialising, particular during the eighteenth century. While Europe's global influence was spreading, China became preoccupied, or perhaps enchanted, with its past glories. The Imperial Qing government became self-satisfied with China's archaic economy. Weakened by internal turmoil, discontent, and corruption, the affluent and exclusive Imperial Court had little interest in accepting anything from the West, let alone industrial technology. At the same time, China's rich business opportunities were tempting many European nations to look East. A contest between the Qing government and the West over whether China's trade door should be opened or closed to the world inevitably occurred. The Qing government lost every battle. Hong Kong's emergence as a British Crown Colony, and the burning of the Imperial Palace in Beijing by an army composed of eight Western countries, was evidence of a bitterly humiliated China.

In 1793, King George III of Britain sent a senior emissary on a deputation to the Court of Emperor Qianlong in Beijing to request the use of an off-shore island depot as a potential trading base with China. The deputation was treated coldly. The Qing Government largely refused to open its door to foreign trade, with the exception of small-scale operations in Guangdong Province. Despite this setback, eighteenth- and nineteenth-century British commerce with China increased fifteen-fold in favour of China, mostly in the trade of silk and tea. This negative balance of trade was a constant problem for the British. In the early nineteenth century Britain seized on an 'imaginative' solution. They began exporting opium to China. The tragedy of the opium trade was immediately obvious. As the drug poured into China, and as the number of opium addicts rapidly increased, British opium merchants and others became wealthy and influential. Meanwhile, China was distracted morally, socially and economically. The Qing government's response to this challenge was to abruptly end most trading activities with the West and firmly closed China's door to the outside world. The Imperial Chinese Court arrogantly rejected all outside influence, vigorously pursuing a policy of commercial and cultural isolation.

In 1840 this isolation was challenged by military means. The humiliation visited on the Chinese people during the so-called Opium Wars demonstrated the clear military and technological superiority of the West. The shame of this period was made even more acute by the fact that China was carved up by some nineteen foreign countries as they joined the scramble for spheres of influence, concessions and protectorates in the ten years before the final collapse of the Qing Dynasty in 1911. These nations included Britain, France, The United States, Russia and Japan, but also lesser players such as Peru, Brazil and Mexico, who all concluded hostilities with China by signing unequal treaties that guaranteed open access to Chinese markets. (It was probably only because of the jealousy and mutual antipathy of competing foreign imperialists that China was spared the type of partition that saw the African continent divided into colonial vassal states).

China realised that it must appropriate Western technological expertise if it was to maintain any vestige of economic power, military advantage or basic sovereignty. Chinese merchants from Fujian Province first responded by importing processing equipment from the West in 1861 in an attempt to value-add to their chief export commodity, tea. From 1861 official Chinese government merchants began purchasing all manner of advanced equipment in order to lay the foundations for a modern industrial society.

Railways, shipping, communications and manufacturing expertise were all a part of this drive towards modernisation, but what most interested the Qing Government was acquiring vast quantities of Western military technology in order to prepare a defence against the West. Ironically, this was part of what become know as the 'Self-Strengthening Movement', a positive response to the earlier isolationist policies of the Qing Dynasty and an attempt to re-open the door to international trade. It was also an attempt to protect China's sovereignty.

However, this reluctant, open door period between China and the West was not underwritten by mutually beneficial commerce, but rather by Western military force, or 'gun boat diplomacy'. The military pre-eminence of Europe ensured that China was forced into signing a number of unequal treaties, which subsequently resulted in China being divided up into different spheres of foreign influence — British, European, American and Japanese. This humiliating subjugation was compounded by the Japanese military victory in the Sino-Japanese War of 1894, which ended with China's crushing defeat.

The corrupt and incompetent late-Qing Dynasty claimed that the Self-Strengthening Movement had been a failure and that the introduction of Western technology had not saved China from its decline or defeat at the hands of the Japanese military. This led senior state functionaries to argue that traditional Chinese culture was the only effective weapon by which to resist the invasion of foreign powers, ideas, culture, and trade. Traditionalists turned back to ancient practices, political conservatism and a fanatical hatred of the 'foreign devils'. Outside influence was again severely restricted.

The 'Cold War'.

The history of China from the late colonial period until the Chinese Revolution in 1949 is typified by invasion and civil war, with only limited intercourse with the rest of the world. Unfortunately for much of the period since 1949, China and the Western alliance have been engaged in a Cold War, essentially over ideological differences. During this time many Western countries adopted a policy of boycotting trade with communist countries including China. This meant that China was again forced to close her door to the West. This time it was not gunboat diplomacy that sought to re-open the door to Western commerce with China, but rather an economic blockade and political containment that blocked China's access to the commercial advantages enjoyed by other countries. During this period of virtual isolation, a programme of internal reconstruction and industrialisation did actually revitalise the Chinese economy, which experienced an average growth rate of 750 percent between 1949 and 1978. However, China essentially remained quarantined from the fundamental economic re-organisation that was sweeping the rest of the world. This was particularly true of the ten years between 1966 and 1976, during the period of destructive social upheaval known as the Cultural Revolution.

During the Cultural Revolution, domestic commercial activities were tightly controlled by the government, with private business regarded as one of the 'devils' of capitalism. As a result China fell well behind the rest of the world in industry, technology and managerial skills. China's overall standard of living fell. For example, in 1965 the Gross Domestic Product (GDP) of Shanghai was higher than that of Hong Kong. By 1976 Hong Kong's economy towered over that of Shanghai. Clearly the closed door policy, first introduced during the Qing Dynasty, but subsequently imposed during the ·Cold War and the Cultural Revolution, visited backwardness and disaster on China's society and economy.

The Miracle of Economic Development
The Open Door

China's door to international trade swung open again in 1978. However on this occasion the opening of the door was a deliberate policy initiative of a sovereign government, not the result of gunboat diplomacy. The Open Door policy, as initiated by the late Paramount Leader Deng Xiao Ping, was a conscious action, supported by the majority of the Chinese people. Its great achievement was that it comprehensively addressed the mistaken policies of previous governments, even those dating back to the Qing Dynasty. The Chinese people clearly recognised that industrial modernisation, the adoption of advanced methods of agriculture, and the opening up of international trade were the only ways China could assume its place as a modern nation.

Part of this process involved what is now known as 'Mind Liberalisation' — a type of social and ideological change that became the necessary prerequisite for the rapid development of China's modern market economy. Mind Liberalisation, part of the 1978 Open Door reforms, led many policy makers to openly challenge contemporary Stalinist economic doctrines — especially towards the end of the Cultural Revolution. It challenged the pre-eminence of a centralised planned economy, the control of business enterprise by government, the general suppression of commercial activities and the law of absolute averages which discriminated against the concept of profit in commerce. This shift in attitudes has changed the way most Chinese think about business. In the PRC, the majority now acknowledge that commerce can, and does, make a very positive contribution to the nation. A healthy economy, a better standard of living and quality of life for all Chinese, and the security of a confident sovereign state are the result of Mind Liberalisation and an Open Door policy for foreign trade and investment. This consensus of opinion established a stable base on which to construct reform in China. From these foundations China has been able to dramatically absorb new technology and expertise and ultimately compete in the global market place.

Foreign Investment

Attracting foreign capital has been an important aspect of China's new policy thrust. The Chinese Department for Industry and Commerce began accepting the registration of foreign companies and liaison offices in 1980. Today, China is the world's fastest growing economy and one of the world's most attractive markets for capital investment. Major investors are drawn from Japan, Hong Kong (now a special administrative region of the PRC), the United States, Germany, France and Taiwan. Based on a survey by the China State Statistical Bureau (CSSB, 2001), in the period between 1980 and 2000 China attracted a total of US$474.3 billion in capital investment from foreign direct investment (FDI). Moreover, contracted FDI was running at US$ 624 billion up to 2000. The unutilised FDI for the year 2000 was US$ 40.7 billion, an increase of US$ 400 million over 1999. According to a report from the Trade and Development Section of the United Nations, China is now ranked second place in the world, behind the United States, in terms of capital inflow. It is felt that FDI not only attracts financial resources for China's economy, but also generates mutual trade opportunities for both the Chinese market and foreign countries. This in turn brings business knowledge and technology into China.

The central Chinese government strengthened its commitment to the fundamentals of foreign investment in its 'Ninth National Five-Year Plan' (1995-2000). According to this plan, the government intended to attract foreign investment into basic industries by providing investors with a set of most-favoured policies. These areas, include new technology in agriculture, the development of synthetic soil resources, water conservation projects, raw material development, energy production, transportation infrastructure, the environmental industry, telecommunications, the IT industry, machinery upgrades, and the expansion of the electronic and mining industries. Consistent with this, the Chinese government issued two important policy directives in 1997. One gave priority to developing the mid-west region of China through a most-favoured investment policy for both foreign and domestic investors. Another was intended to provide foreign investors with transparent and predictable guidelines that focused on the projects most urgently required by China. Clearly, it is in the best interests of all foreign investors to be familiar with the primary characteristics of the Chinese market and to understand the psychology that underpins this.

Economic Miracle

The reform policies of Deng Xiao Ping have served the goal of economic growth well. China has experienced something of an economic miracle with an annual average growth rate in GDP of 8 per cent over twenty years since 1979. Economic reform has seen China's exports grow from US$18.27 billion in 1980 to US$ 249.2 billion in 2000 (CSSB, 2001), an increase of 13.6 times. China's total imports and exports are presently running at US$ 474.3 billion for the year 2000, representing 4 per cent of the world's total import and export trade — an increase of 69 per cent compared with 1995. This puts China in seventh place overall in the world in terms of imports, and the eighth place overall in terms of exports for the year 2000. With the return of Hong Kong to China, in July 1997, China is now the fourth largest trading country in the world behind the USA, Japan and Germany, with an overall trade surplus of US$ 24.1 billion in 2000 (CSSB, 2001). It is not surprising that China's degree of economic dependency on foreign trade rose to 40 per cent in 1999.

The Chinese government achieved an average 8.3 per cent growth rate of GDP between 1995 and 2000, and has US$393 billion in domestic investment of fixed assets in 2000. China's GDP in 2000 was about US$ 1070 billion, a 41 per cent increase over 1995 with comparable prices. According to the World Bank, China's GDP ranked seventh in the world, with US$780 per capita (GDP) by the end of 1999. This means that China has progressed from a low- to a lower-middle income country in less than ten years. As a result, China's foreign exchange reserve reached US$165.6 billion at the end of 2000 (CSSB, 2001), ranking second in the world after Japan. In 2000, with a growth rate of GDP at 8.0 per cent, China's domestic investment in fixed assets was US$394.4 billion. In addition, China's national resident savings levels reached US$ 767.74 billion in the period up to November 2000, a huge increase from US$ 96.5 billion in 1995. Clearly this high level of domestic savings has provided China with a huge capital base.

China's State Statistical Bureau (2001) reported that the output of many agriculture and industry products was amongst the highest in the world in 1999. For example, the annual output of cotton, oil seed, fish, vegetable, fruit and meat, were on the highest ranking that year. China's annual figures for the production of coal, cement, fertilisers and the manufacture of television sets, similarly lead the world. The annual output of steel has remained in the first rank since 1995, when China overtook the United States. Finally, the annual output of woollens, tea, cotton cloth and electric power was in the second rank of world production.

Based on this rapid level of economic growth, the rate of China's urbanisation is also accelerating. According to a statistical report produced by the Ministry of Construction, the number of cities in China has increased dramatically since 1980. China's urban population has reached 455.94 million, 36.09 per cent of the total population in 1999. There were 664 cities in year 2000, 40 per cent of which are located in eastern China, with a further 37 per cent in central China, and 19 per cent in western China. The country's huge market and the continued trend towards urbanisation will make the PRC even more attractive for trade and investment.

Many foreign companies have contested China's telecommunication market since the early 1990s. Ten million telephones were installed nation wide in 1994. During this period, the total number of new connections in China was twice the total number of existing telephones in Hong Kong. In comparison, although possessing the largest number of actual telephones in the world, the greatest number of new connections in any one year in the United States stands at only 7 million. This means that China now outranks the USA in terms of the highest number of new telephone connections in any one year. In 2000, there were on average 280,000 new telephone installations per day in China. There were 140 million telephone users or holders and over 90 million mobile phone customers registered in China by the end of 2000. During the same period, there were approximately 16.9 million Internet users in China with 6.5 million computers connected to the Internet. According to 'The PRC Desk Top PC Market Report of 1997', produced by the Huicong Group (the largest private marketing research company in China), the total selling volume of personal computers (PCs) in China in the first half of 1997 was 1,431,000 units. The report estimated that China's annual selling PC volume would be over 3,100,000 units by the end of 1997, an increase of 61 per cent on the previous year's total selling volume.

An IMF study found that much of China's economic growth since 1978 has been due to increases in productivity. This is not only because of improvements in technology, but also because of an increase in capital expenditure and labour output. This has lead to a reallocation of labour into higher value-added activities. Even in township and village enterprises, private-owned operations are encouraged to focus on the bottom line. Investment in joint ventures and foreign enterprises has further led to an improvement in management effectiveness and increased productivity.

The late twentieth century saw two former colonies returned to China. Hong Kong's turnover to China took place in 1997. Macau was returned to China in 1999. These cities are now both considered Special Administration Regions. Their return has definitely reinforced China's level of economic growth.

China in the Twenty-First Century
A Real Market

In twenty years, China has undergone a complete transformation from a sleeping, introvert giant, into a dynamic global force. This has lead the Organisation for Economically Developed Countries (OECD) to predict that by 2015 China will surpass the United States as the world's largest purchaser of goods and services. While this prediction may be over optimistic, however this indicate that China will continue to grow and play a unique role in world trade.

In looking for evidence to support this optimistic projection, the industriousness of the Chinese people is a key critical factor. Another is China's relatively high level of general education, particularly in urban areas, as well as an enviable national savings programme, which is over twice the average rate of most Western nations. Nevertheless, the main reason why international business is fascinated with the Chinese market is that China possesses 26 per cent of the world's population. China's population is in fact more than the sum of the populations of the European Union (EU) and the North American Free Trade Agreement (NAFTA). There are 335 million people in the EU and 360 million in NAFTA. Currently, the population of China is 1.3 billion, the world's largest market.

Clearly this market is taken seriously by the West. China's economic growth has been fuelled by a massive inflow of foreign capital and expertise. Although the absolute output of many Chinese industries is among the highest in the world, China's per capita net income and output of high-tech products, such as cars, computers, telephones, mobile phones are far lower than those of developed countries. Thus there is an enormous potential market in China for both domestic and foreign companies and many foreign companies and MNCs have established subsidiaries in the PRC. Most of the world's corporate flagships are now represented in China. In addition, many western-based, overseas Chinese-owned companies are now operating successfully in the PRC. These well-connected entrepreneurs, who were practically excluded from any commercial activity in China before 1978, have established close ties with their ancestral homeland. This international network of Chinese capital has further diversified and strengthened the economy of the PRC.

There is, however, a degree of scepticism about China's economic growth from the period of the early 1980s up until the present. Some so-called 'experts' argue that China's huge population does not necessarily mean that its market is attractive for international investment and that low labour costs do not guarantee a desirable destination for FDI. According to them, China does not have a large enough middle class to absorb a commercially viable volume of consumer goods, with most of the population classified as poor. It is also said that China does not have enough people with appropriate management skills and sufficient legal protection to guarantee a desirable business environment for Sino-foreign joint ventures. However, China's economic performance in recent years and the fact that an increasing number of MNCs now operate lucrative businesses in China, have disproved many of these arguments. According to the current CEO of Nokia, China is the telecommunication giant's second most important global market, with sales in China worth US$2.8 billion for the year 2000. This positive view is supported by the comments of a top International CEO who remarked that without solid strategies in China, you will not be able to lead your company into globalisation (Lian, 2001). The decision of the International Olympic Committee to award Beijing the 2008 Summer Games is also evidence of this optimism. The IOC's decision will expose China to a second 'great opening', where business infrastructure reform and social development will continue to drive investment.

The World Trade Organisation Effect

One of the most exciting commercial prospects for the business world in the early twenty-first century is China's entry into the

World Trade Organisation (WTO). It will bring opportunities, risks, losses and fortune to different groups and classes of enterprise in China, both foreign and domestic, and it is a significant milestone in China's economic development.

China's WTO entry will create even more business opportunities for foreign companies doing business in China, especially for MNCs. The basic aims of WTO entry for China is to lower tariffs, ban trade-blockade policies on both exports and imports, and open new markets among fellow WTO members in the Chinese market. China must slash tariffs on many imported products, including cars, and agricultural products, so that foreign companies are able to compete equally in the Chinese market and win positive business benefits by exploiting various competitive advantages. This will inevitably lessen the Chinese Government's control over China's foreign trade. Even prior to WTO, China strongly indicated to the world that she welcomed FDI, though there were still restrictions in place for the foreign investor. Entry into WTO will minimise impediments for foreign companies who wish to invest in China. China's car industry, retail market, telecommunication industry (including Internet and IT industries), financing services, insurance services and fund management will all be opened up to outside investment and it is anticipated that these measures will result in a surge in the number of foreign companies looking to set up manufacturing plants (Whelan, 2001).

There are a number of other positive expectations associated with China's entry intro WTO. Firstly, it is believed that it will further facilitate China's export growth, especially in textiles, hardware products, machines, and electronic goods. Secondly, China's rights will be protected through WTO if there is a trade dispute between China and another country. At the same time,

China will no longer be concerned about whether one of its largest export destinations, namely the United States, grants the status of Most Favourable Nation (MFN) on an annual basis. Thirdly, the performance and standard of services of domestic enterprises will be pushed to effectively improve, as a result of increased international competition in the Chinese market. Accordingly, this will promote China's commercial reform and lead Chinese enterprises towards greater efficiency, effectiveness and competitiveness in the global market. Higher quality goods should then appear in local markets.

The prices of some important goods and services, such as cars and telecommunications services, which were previously monopolised by the Chinese Government, will be reduced by having more foreign players competing in the game. Likewise, Chinese consumers should enjoy an increased range of quality financial services. Finally, China's entry to WTO will have a positive social impact on Chinese society. Job opportunities for skilled workers and business people will be increased, as a result of more FDI flowing in to China. This will drive the growth and confidence of the middle-class. The growing business class will hold the power to demand the protection of effective law enforcement. It has even been predicted that corruption will be dramatically reduced, as local officials will have much less power to control the activities of local enterprises, while business operations will follow rules and regulations under the monitoring eye of the WTO. The official licensing and approval of business operations and tariffs will also decrease.

Besides promising prosperity, there are also vital threats to China's industries and to Chinese society (Lai and Ye, 1999). Whether China can significantly benefit from joining WTO, depends on how it manages tough challenges from the outside world. Under WTO rules, an open and freely competitive market must substitute for an administrative system that protects local business interests. Some of China's most important national industries, especially low performers, will be facing potentially fatal threats without government protection. Many local enterprises, especially low performing state-owned enterprises (SOE) will go out of business if they cannot compete with international giants in their particular area of commerce. For the same reason, some industries, which have come to symbolise the struggle of nation building, may be driven out of business for good, and several well-known Chinese consumer brands could disappear from the market. Unemployment in SOEs and the public sector will increase sharply. Limited-skill workers, in both urban and rural areas, will lose their jobs. Disaffected, under-utilised or under-employed workers may become a source of great social unrest. This is in fact one of the Chinese Central Government's biggest concerns, namely that fundamental changes in the social structure could have a negative impact on economic development and usher in a serious challenge to the administration of government.

Clearly, China's exposure to international competition has already indirectly increased the productivity and growth of local enterprises through exports. As the process of globalisation increases China's WTO entry will aid this process still further.

Chapter 2

Traditional Chinese Business Values

Western and Chinese cultural values have different origins. The West has nurtured the concept of relative social equality. The entire Chinese social system is based on inequality, where values have contingent meanings within different social contexts. Chinese egalitarianism focuses on equal results rather than equal opportunities. This arose because Chinese civilisation developed around the common interests of the agrarian-based family, not the individual. The foundations of Chinese civilisation are autocratic, unequal and hierarchical in terms of seniority, and not at all democratic. These distinctions cannot be understood by simplistic interpretations of Confucian history or ideology. Confucianism's primary objective of implementing a basic theory of how to govern has been redefined by the social consensus of the Open Door policy. Business culture in modern China can only be understood as a core of ancient norms grafted onto sets of uniquely contemporary and complementary values. China has in fact discovered a workable détente between the need for social stability and demands of profound change. In this chapter the importance of hierarchy as defined by five basic human relationship categories is explained. The role and function of these relationships are further illustrated by examining collectivism orientation and the various social manifestations of 'Face'. The emerging values of modern Chinese business culture are contrasted against the ancient values of modesty and humility, respect for and a desire to follow, tradition, egalitarianism, an emphasis on agriculture as opposed to commerce, and the way in which modern Chinese businesspeople have dealt with the traditional social norm of limiting the pursuit of personal wealth.

Confucian Predominance

Confucius was born in the small state of Lu, which is located in modern-day Shandong Province, around 2500 B.C. This was a time of absolute political and social turmoil and the cornerstone of Confucianism concerns the governance of a nation. Based on his ideas, the belief system we know as Confucianism became the dominant cultural influence in China for over 3000 years.

Confucianism maintains that 'moral convention' is the cement that binds society together. In the case of China, convention can be deconstructed into six major areas of influence, which in turn can be seen as constituting the foundations of traditional Chinese society. They are hierarchy, collectivism, 'face', pragmatism, high uncertainty avoidance, and egalitarianism. An appreciation of these values is fundamental to any study of Chinese national values and their influence on ways of doing business today.

Hierarchy

Traditional Chinese culture is characterised by hierarchy. Many studies of Chinese social organisation have demonstrated that China gives greater weight to hierarchy than most Western countries (Hofested, 1980; Cheung and Chow, 1999). Chinese culture accepts social inequality in terms of the hierarchical ordering of society. This is because Western and Chinese cultural values have different origins. For many reasons, historical, socio-cultural and religious, the West has nurtured the concept of relatively social equality. Particular instances include equality 'in the sight of God' and in the case of American civilisation, equal opportunity in every field of human endeavour, including commerce. Over time this has created the cultural and psychological basis for a democratic consciousness.

In contrast, Chinese cultural values derive from a civilisation that originated in a continental environment and prospered through agriculture rather than maritime trade. Chinese civilisation developed around the common interests of the family as the pre-eminent economic unit, not the city-state, and certainly not the individual. Chinese culture is actually built on the 'family state', a form of social organisation that is autocratic, unequal and hierarchical in terms of seniority, and not at all democratic (Feng, 1985).

Responding to the social turmoil of the period, Confucianism provided a basic theory of how to govern a troubled nation. Confucianism maintains that only a distinct hierarchy, in which each level of society is obedient to the level above it, can guarantee the stability of a country and safeguard the power of the ultimate ruler. In Confucianism, the internal hierarchy of the patriarchal family, which arose from China's traditional agricultural economy, is used as a model to support a hierarchical social order. Confucius identified five basic human relationship categories, which he called '*Wu Lun*'. They are as follows: Emperor (kindness)/ Subject (loyalty); Father (support and consideration) / Son (Piety and obedience); Husband (protection)/ Wife (submission); Older Brother (care)/ Younger Brother (modelling subject); and lastly, Friends or Friendship (trust and obligation). A traditional Chinese saying maintains that 'If an Emperor asks a subject to forfeit his life, then the subject must do so without question; and a son must sacrifice himself, if his father asks him to do so.'

Five Basic Human Relationship Categories ('*Wu Lun*') of Confucianism

Relationship	Representing	With	Representing
Emperor	Kindness	Subject	Loyalty
Father	Support & Consideration	Son	Piety & Obedience
Husband	Protection	Wife	Submission
Older brother	Care	Younger brother	Modelling subject
Friend	Trust & Obligation	Friend	Trust & Obligation

Confucianism justifies the ethical significance of a hierarchical system by claiming that these relations should be governed by a number of key moral norms. These include loyalty (*zhong*); piety (*xiao*); kindness (*ren*); obligation (*yi*); codes of hierarchy (*li*). Codes of hierarchy (*li*) are the core of the system. They require that everyone strictly comply with these norms in order to confirm his or her status within a specific social class. The upper classes require that lower classes demonstrate loyalty to them, while lower classes expect that persons of high status show them kindness in return for their loyalty. The untoward consequence of social carelessness, in respect to a breakdown in these relationships, is condemnation or sanction. Confucianism holds that rulers can effectively control the whole of society, and even the natural environment, through a strict adherence to these well-defined norms. Over two thousand years of Chinese history clearly demonstrates a consistent implementation of this belief system.

Nowadays in China this deeply-rooted sense of hierarchy is still evident at all levels of society. Most Chinese people still accept inequality, both in their social life and in the workplace. This is equally true in respect to wealth, power, social status and rights. Whether it would be superiors and subordinates at work, or senior state officials and ordinary members of the public, the essentially unequal nature of social relations is recognised by one and all. The entire Chinese social system is based on existential inequality. Subordinates, or 'ordinary people', expect to be told what to do. Politics in the PRC, and the machinations of the Chinese bureaucracy and commercial enterprises, are practically incomprehensible without first understanding this key point.

All Confucian principles are ultimately based on this notion of a social hierarchy. Collectivism, or interdependence, is built upon a hierarchical social framework, which means that individuals must show loyalty to the hierarchical ordering of society. Similarly, respect for tradition requires that everyone follow the norms and values stipulated by elders or persons in authority. 'Face' ensures that everyone is sensitive to each other's position in the hierarchical system, while egalitarianism stresses that people should be satisfied with their equal economic status within the same social rank without challenging authority. Essentially, the basic differentiation between Chinese and Western cultural values originates in this dynamic. Some Westerners have tried to familiarise themselves with these dimensions of the Chinese cultural framework, including the values of collectivism and 'face', but still complain that they find Chinese culture confusing. This is because many non-Chinese do not appreciate that these values have contingent or different meanings depending on their context within the social hierarchy.

Collectivism

In Chinese culture, collectivism defines individual status. Individuals are not defined by independent status as such but by their dependent relations within the social hierarchy. This differs from individualistic cultures in which people are encouraged, and indeed expected, to look after their own interests and those of their immediate, or nuclear family (Hofstede, 1980). Rather, the culture of Confucianism prefers that individual members of society, as a dependent part of a social whole, demonstrate their loyalty to particular groups with the hierarchical system, such as the extended family, work organisation or ultimately society as a whole. It emphasises the importance of maintaining harmonious interpersonal relationships. In meeting this requirement a person should act in accordance with external expectations rather than with his or her own internal wishes or desires. Traditional cultural values maintain that any manifestation of independent motives, such as competition with, or distinction from, others is self-seeking and destructive. It is in fact considered selfish and immoral. This cultural orientation is reflected in ordinary Chinese people's desire to avoid competition. Importantly, it also leads positively to a sense of group solidarity and is reflected in today's business world in areas such as negotiation, business networking, teamwork and cooperation.

In a wider cultural sense, traditional Chinese concepts of collectivism mean that a 'one-man' domination system prevails with subordinates contributing their loyalty and commitment. In this scheme of things the person at the summit of the social hierarchy possesses absolute authority with everyone under him or her assuming a level of dependence on his or her superior authority. Giving up individual interests in favour of a higher social prerogative is considered to be an essential quality of the Confucian ideal of the 'perfect personality'. The Confucian 'ethical man' is more than only morally just (Fang, 1985), he or she also should be a cooperating member of the hierarchical society. Confucianism does not conceive of individuals as existing separately from the social structure, but as ethical components of a greater whole. This characteristic differentiates the Chinese concept of collectivism from Western collectivism in that it emphasises members' equal cooperation and interdependence.

The Many Faces Of 'Face'

Face is a both an ancient traditional norm and a current social value in China. 'Face' is a concept that is not uniquely held by Chinese people. It has universal applicability. However, it is grounded in webs of interpersonal and socio-cultural variability. In Western society, the concept of 'face' is mostly related to personal ability, or to competence and personality (Arkin & Sheppard, 1989; Bond & Hwang, 1986), whereas in China, 'face' is situationally defined in terms of self-image (Alexander & Knight, 1971; Goffman, 1955). 'Face' in China not only deals with relationships between one's own status or image and public acceptance, but is also delicately involved in *relationships between individuals*. Chinese people are strongly concerned with how to protect or enhance both theirs *and others'* 'face'. One of the most fundamental and enduring distinctions between China and the West in respect to 'face' is that a 'loss of face' in the West is associated with internalised feelings, such as guilt. This reflects an individual or social orientation (Goodfellow, Smith & O'Neill, 1999). On the other hand, in China a 'loss of face' is a form of public humiliation resulting in shame — a distinctly collective, or rather communal sentiment.

It is generally argued that 'face' is evident in all aspects of Chinese life and that the Chinese concept refers not only to a person's private affairs, but also to a person's entire extended family, social networks, and community at large (Fang, 1999; Wang, Zhang & Goodfellow,

1998). Importantly, in Chinese culture, concern with 'face' is relationship-oriented. In China, any 'face-enhancing' activity must be based on principles of either respecting higher status or reciprocating with others at a peer level.

There are numerous common expressions describing 'face' relationships in Chinese culture. They include the following: 'losing face', 'hurting face', 'protecting face', 'giving face' or 'enhancing face' (namely elevating someone's esteem and reputation), 'wanting face' (namely desiring self-esteem within relationships), 'struggling for face', and 'having face' (i.e. being respected by others).

In the Chinese cultural context, there must be reciprocal obligations at the peer level. That is to say, all relationships between friends, relatives or colleagues must be reciprocal. Practically, this means one must do one's best to reciprocate a favour. The untoward consequence of social carelessness in respect to repaying a favour may be a 'loss of face' or 'hurt face'. Most importantly, 'face work' is about building and maintaining a relationship between oneself and people of a higher or lower social scales. When something affects the individual's standing or reputation, then it has both upward and downward social ramifications. Associated with the notion of hierarchy, 'face protection' means that a person should meet the social or personal requirements of superiors and seniors. Accordingly, an individual is obliged to demonstrate unqualified cooperation after properly identifying his or her self-modesty in terms of personal status within the system. From a Chinese point of view, 'face work' within a hierarchical context is a necessary precondition for any individual to function appropriately within society. A person of relative lower social standing must be sensitive to the social requirements of those higher on the social scale by 'face enhancing'. They must also be aware of the absolute importance of authority.

The failure of non-Chinese to appreciate this within the context of a public relationship often leads indirectly to a sense of social awkwardness or embarrassment on the part of Chinese associates or hosts in terms of 'face' concerns.

Interestingly, when 'face work' is used in Chinese society for enhancing one's influence over others, it is not like what people in the West understand as improving one's own social standing. In Western society, to enhance 'face', people often arrange the setting for social interaction. They then behave in a specific manner in order to shape an appropriate and attractive image when dealing with others from a different class (Bond & Hwang, 1986). Enhancing 'face' in Chinese society means that a person with higher prestige strongly expects people with lower status to add to his or her 'face', by presenting compliments or gifts and conforming to his or her opinions and behaviour. For example, a subordinate would assume that his or her boss had extended 'special face' if the boss requested a favour of them after office hours. This request would be interpreted as meaning one of two things. First, that the boss trusted him or her more than others, and second, that the boss was closer to him or her than other employees. In both cases the experience would be considered positive and beneficial. Refusal to cooperate would hurt the boss's 'face' and may even bring about a negative result in the employee's career. A refusal of this type is not just a refusal of a favour *per se,* but the rejection of a relationship. 'Face protection' is an essential stitch in the rich tapestry of Chinese business culture. Its influence can be seen in every aspect of leadership style, of customer psychology and negotiation strategy. In recent years, confusion over this concept has led to many grave misunderstandings between China and the West. These topics will be raised in more detail in subsequent chapters.

Case Study: Losing Face versus Losing Opportunity

Some Western businessmen once spent a million dollars to buy a round of cappuccinos because they failed to recognise the importance of 'face' in Chinese culture. The situation indirectly arose from a high-level foreign business delegation to the People's Republic of China. Their host, who was the managing director of one of the PRC's largest diversified conglomerates, lavished five-star hospitality on the visitors. The itinerary included several introductions to senior trade, industry and political figures, as well as a series of intimate 'get to know you' sightseeing excursions with executives of a newly-privatised, state-owned enterprise, hungry for modern expertise and materials.

A reciprocal visit was organised. The foreign directors picked up the Chinese delegation at the airport, stopped for a quick coffee and rushed to make the important nine o'clock meeting. This was so that they could get right get down to business. This proved to be the most expensive round of cappuccinos in history. The Chinese delegation was polite. They agreed with everything. Then they left on the first available flight. On arriving home, the Chinese side immediately exercised their option to withdraw their US$1,000,000 in venture capital.

What had happened here was that the managing director of the Chinese delegation had lost 'face' in front of his subordinates. He had boasted to them before leaving China of the good character of the Westerners. He was in fact eagerly anticipating the opportunity to get to know his new partners and to enjoy some reciprocal hospitality — to go fishing, play golf and get his picture taken at some of the local tourist attractions. The Chinese delegation's visit was as much about codes of hierarchy as it was about business opportunities. It was intended to demonstrate that the Chinese director was a person worthy of reciprocal hospitality, though it had little to do with hospitality *per se*. The purpose of his visit was to improve his standing in the eyes of his own delegation, to fortify his decision to proceed with the joint venture, and to get to know the character of the people he was planing to do business with. Against these imperatives 'the big 9:00 am meeting' was of little consequence. Failure to appreciate the importance of hierarchy resulted in the senior Chinese member of the delegation losing 'face' and ultimately to the disintegration of the entire project. What the director felt was a sense of shame at the careless treatment that he received on his first morning in a Western country. It left him with no alternative but to immediately move to re-establish his position in the hierarchy by placing his reputation above short-term material benefits. The result was a failure ultimately for the Western side, but not for the Chinese who were able to attract the attention of another investor who had a well-disciplined and trained team of China specialists to advise them on protocol and strategies.

Pragmatism: *Human Nature, the Supernatural*

Subjective, non-empirical concepts such as human nature are also an important dimension of cross-cultural management. Most cultures view people as either essentially good or essentially evil, or sometimes a mixture of the two. Some Western researchers misunderstand this dimension of Chinese culture by arguing that Confucianism maintains that human nature is basically good. They also argue that Western culture asserts that human nature is essentially flawed and that the result of sin, in terms of the Christian religion, is evil (Kluckhorn and Strodtbeck, 1961). Theoretically, a more autocratic style is likely to rule in countries that focus on the evil side of people, while a participatory-style government should appeal to countries that emphasise the good side of human beings (Robbins et al, 1994). One could find, however, that rather more is involved here than simply a comparative extrapolation between the virtues of differing value systems — i.e. between Western values and Confucianism — as there is a difficulty in matching practice with simplistic interpretations of Confucian ideology. In reality, Chinese leadership tends to be more autocratic than that of many Western countries (Wang and Clegg, 2002). Authoritarianism prevails in China, while paradoxically democracy flourishes in the West, where man is held to be inherently wicked!

Actually, Confucianism believes that although human nature is initially good, it is inevitably subject to social and family influence. People become 'bad' if exposed to evil influences — for example, human beings easily become greedy when placed in the wrong environment. Confucianism therefore argues that because men and woman have the potential to become evil, the only way to prevent this from happening is a strict adherence to moral principles and hierarchical regulations. Tight hierarchical social control becomes a practical necessity. Consequently, in traditional Chinese culture, it is believed that behaviour should be positively influenced and ruled by Heaven or by Heaven's representative — the Emperor.

Confucianism does not accept the existence of ghosts or apparitions, but it does believe in Heaven. In ancient China an Emperor ruled by a heavenly mandate. Hence, the Emperor was referred to as the 'son of Heaven', and represented Heaven in order to control and lead people in their worldly society (In traditional China, a woman was not entitled to rank and was therefore referred to under her son's title or name).

Although the followers of Confucius believe that much of life is predestined, they are also encouraged to participate in the secular world. Confucianism provides ethical guidelines on how to pursue a successful career by linking a person's normal life to Heaven's will through the cultivation of the positive aspects of human nature, especially in politics and the secular world. This doctrine differs greatly from traditional Taoism, which argues that an ideal personal life-style should not be concerned with worldly affairs; instead, the search for internal peace and harmony should be the single preoccupation of a good man or woman. In a sense, Confucianism is pragmatic in that it encourages people to be involved in society in proper accordance with their specific social status (Feng, 1985). Confucianism stresses that people should and will succeed in their careers if they follow Heaven's will and cultivate good human nature. It links the super-natural with practical doctrines through human nature. This may be a reason why many Chinese do not easily abandon a secular life, such as making money, while in pursuit of a spiritual life, and why they adopt very pragmatic and flexible approaches to business. In other words a secular life is justified by Confucian pragmatic philosophy.

High Uncertainty Avoidance

Another characteristic feature of Confucianism is 'high uncertainty avoidance' (Cheung and Chow, 1999). Confucianism argues that respect for tradition and 'middle-stand' orientation (or the doctrine of the mean) are an effective way to avoid uncertainty in life.

Modesty and Humility. Confucianism believes that an effective way to minimise social uncertainty is to follow 'the doctrine of the mean' — the middle way. This concerns extremes of behaviour or opinions, including socially careless action. There are many traditional Chinese norms that reflect this value, including a prohibition against demonstrations of public aggression, excessive individualism, competition, or risk taking. This social norm still prevails in Chinese society. Most people try to avoid directly confrontation with others, including the use of explicit words or comments. Most people will even avoid using words such as 'very good' or 'very bad' in formal matters, in order to avoid any risk of 'face damage'. Rather, the Chinese believe that the best way to express oneself is to be modest and humble.

Respect for and a desire to follow tradition. Confucianism advocates that people should follow the rules set by the Emperor, the representative of Heaven (Feng, 1985). As a philosophy it maintains that it is dangerous to transgress these rules. In a society with high uncertainty avoidance, people feel threatened by ambiguity, so mechanisms and norms are created to provide security and reduce risk. In traditional China, there was a low tolerance for deviant ideas and behaviours, and social condemnation and punishment awaited anyone who acted against the norms of society or contravened the rules. Faithfully following traditional rules is believed to be the best way to avoid uncertainty. Before the reforms of 1978, Chinese people had held a strong orientation towards the past. In traditional China, first-order preference was given to both the study of history and ancestor veneration. This meant that the ideas of elders and predecessors were thought of as practically imperial edicts. It was strongly maintained that the younger generation must follow regulations established by the 'aged'. More often than not this group was identified as the 'older generation'.

In this veneration of elders, both the strength and weakness of the Chinese social system are revealed. In the first instance, authority was synonymous with tradition and tradition dictated automatic deference to hierarchy — a form of circular logic. In a positive sense this approach has produced the longest continuous civilisation in human history. However, in this stability lies the Chinese social system's greatest weakness. Because deviant behaviour is not tolerated, ironclad mores lead to a debilitating incapacity to adapt, to innovate or to change. This cultural orientation means that the Chinese adhere strictly to convention. Convention in this sense is similar to the religious obligations of people in the monotheistic West. In traditional China, convention was practically a religious value.

Misunderstandings about the Chinese notion of respect for tradition originate from differing ideas or perspectives about religion. Chinese people practice ancestor worship while most Western people are exclusive God-worshippers. These differences in the focus of veneration result in a significant difference in mental outlook. Exclusive God-worshipers believe that God is transcendent. This belief leads people to think that moral principles originate in the spiritual world and that these are completely separate from managerial principles in the worldly workplace (Pascale and Athos, 1981). People holding this view easily accept a concept by which management formulates dynamic practical demands in the workplace rather than falls back on unchangeable traditional moral law. Ancestor worshipers on the other hand, believe that the younger generation should adore the family founder as the font of moral authority.

The main characteristics of ancestor worship are that, first, the object of worship is based on the secular rather than on the supernatural world. Second, that ancestor worship is related to particular persons of particular ages in a family or social structure — the more senior an individual is in terms of age, the more power or respect should be accorded him (or her). Finally, the heritage of moral law must be followed in worldly affairs once it has been established by the elders. The consequence of this world-view is that Chinese people venerate a secular authority that has a direct association with social standing and hierarchy. It was believed that this approach guaranteed that there was no risk of turmoil within families, communities and the nation as a whole, both in the present and the future.

While Chinese ancestor veneration has weakened in recent years, the worship of tradition (the extension of ancestor worship) still plays a major role in many organisations. Most elderly Chinese still believe that tradition cannot be, and should not be, neglected.

Egalitarianism

Egalitarianism is an important aspect of Confucianism. The meaning of this value is, however, very different from the concept in Western culture. Chinese egalitarianism focuses on equal results rather than equal opportunities. Confucianism maintains that society would be more stable if wealth and income were allocated equally within a single and constant economic and social system. A Chinese wise saying maintains 'Do not worry that people are poor, but rather be concerned if wealth is not allocated equally'. According to this value, Chinese egalitarianism is a form of 'shared poverty'. According to Confucianism, people should accept their poverty, rank or position within the hierarchy, and not challenge the political or hierarchical structure. This consciousness remains deeply embedded in Chinese culture, even in the present day.

Ancient Business Values

As argued, Confucianism has constituted the ideological engine of almost every aspect of Chinese society for more than two thousand years. It has profoundly contributed to the development of Chinese business culture.

Valuing Agriculture and Belittling Commerce

China has always been an agrarian-based society. In traditional agricultural societies, almost all goods were produced for subsistence consumption or for the payment of state taxes in kind. Generally speaking, Chinese governments throughout history have based most of their policies around support for agriculture. This support has always occurred at the expense of mercantile activities. The traditional Chinese value of attaching importance to agriculture and 'belittling' commerce has retarded China's potential as a major trading nation for over 2,000 years. Confucianism argues that the objective of state power is to maintain social stability. Agriculture is believed to be the base of social stability because it restricts people to fixed geographical areas based on food production. Politically, it makes people easier to govern and to control. Traditionally, Chinese rulers believed that the mobility of commercial activities could potentially undermine stability. Furthermore, commercial transactions could only result in individual benefit, not wealth for society in general. Consequently the Chinese possess a very poor historical appreciation of the principles of commodity exchange. Confucianism emphasises that a moral person should be concerned with righteousness and benevolence rather than with benefits.

This value discriminates against the accumulation of wealth through commerce. It requires Chinese businesspeople to place more emphasis on moral, rather than economic, benefits. This sentiment still exists in China's developing market economy.

Many Chinese entrepreneurs in fact like to be seen to enthusiastically sponsor various benevolent or philanthropic public projects. Good publicity, or rather public relations, will establish a person's Confucianist moral credentials against allegations of individualistic profit seeking.

Business: *Crafty and Unscrupulous*

Confucian culture has had a low regard for business in the past. According to Chinese tradition, there are four social classes — officials and intellectuals; peasants; workers; and finally, at the bottom of the heap, businessmen. The businessperson, ranked at the bottom of the society, is regarded by Confucianism as the 'mean man' (*xiao ren*). Confucianism stresses that 'the superior man' understands righteousness (*yi*), whereas the 'miserable man' merely comprehends benefits (*li*). A decent person focuses on kindness, whilst a 'base' man focuses on personal profits or interests. Chinese tradition generally regards the merchant as an unscrupulous person. This does not mean that Confucianism has not accommodated business into its moral code. In practice, the purpose of commerce in China was to be found in the long-term enrichment and subsequent preservation of the family unit. This is a key point on which later discussions of modern Chinese business values will be based.

Before 1978, this traditional value strongly influenced Chinese people's belief that commerce was a base occupation. In traditional Chinese culture most Chinese intellectuals pursued careers as officials of the ruling class. A career in commerce was an imprudent career option. In traditional Chinese society, to engage in business was to invite contempt. Mind Liberalisation and the benefits of China's Open Door policy has meant that the influence of this value has now weakened.

Limiting the Pursuit of Personal Wealth

Traditional Chinese values condemn self-actualisation and over-emphasise non-individual elements of social organisation. Confucianism argues that all forms of self-promotion, such as exerting one's personality in the workplace, will cause people to compete to further their own selfish interests. Confucianism regards selfishness as the root of all evil. The accumulation of personal wealth through commerce — regarded as a form of selfishness — was afforded a low priority in Chinese traditional society. Anyone who directly indicated an interest in money and wealth was thought to be either mean or of low character. In pre-modern Chinese society, peasants, who incidentally still make up the great mass of the Chinese population, upheld the virtue of, 'being satisfied with things as they are'. The discouragement of competition existed in all areas of Chinese social life and the individual pursuit of wealth was limited by this ethic.

This negative Confucian value was extensively promoted during the Cultural Revolution of 1966-1976. During this time, the Chinese Government prohibited all forms of private enterprise, regarding business as the 'tail of the capitalist beast [which] needed to be cut off'. For this reason competitive commercial behaviour in contemporary China can only be dated back to 1978.

We have now established the important point that knowledge of traditional Chinese cultural values is vital to a proper understanding of Chinese business culture and specific social behavioural patterns. Correctly applied, it is an important tool for building confidence in doing business in China and for understanding the context in which many of China's fundamental economic and social reforms have taken place. Practically, this knowledge should form the basis of any strategy aimed at avoiding a clash of cultures.

Chapter 3

The Revolution in Chinese Business

Since 1978, Deng Xiao Ping's Open Door policy has challenged many traditional cultural assumptions. This has opened the minds of Chinese people to the economic and social benefit of 'Capitalism with a Chinese face'. This chapter explains how in one generation a 3000-year antipathy to commerce was transformed into a general acceptance that business was a worthy vocation. In China, success in business now reflects the efficient and equitable use of resources. This new value has been combined with long-standing concepts that emphasises friendly cooperation as the basis for success, including the notion that personal relationships play a pre-eminent role in business and that friendship networks, or *guanxi*, reduces both risk and competition. A central theme is that *guanxi* relationships hold a value that is considered superior to money. The use of stratagems and tactics developed over thousands of years, also shows that business relations in China are complex, but rational. They are based on the ability to accept the realities of a market economy and the global business environment, the necessity to adapt to competition by professional knowledge, imagination, skill and strategy, and the wisdom to adopt those values best able to produce a positive outcome, not only for the individual businessperson, but also for the nation. This chapter examines the modern day value of '*being rich is glorious*', and compares this to the long-standing and still relevant belief in the 'seamlessness' of business and officialdom.

In the last chapter it was argued that prior to 1978, certain traditional values actually held back the development of commerce and trade in China. It is beyond dispute that since then the situation has changed dramatically largely because Deng Xiao Ping's Open Door policy created the possibility of challenging many traditional cultural and economic assumptions. Some of these changes may be attributed to Chinese exposure to Western influences as a result of joint ventures with foreign companies — a kind of cultural cross-fertilisation. They are also a consequence of the global expansion of various forms of technology, including the electronic media. Many people believe that change is simply part of the evolution of a uniquely Chinese system of commerce. Whatever the causes, Chinese people recognise that economic and social reforms have brought real benefit. Moreover, what is equally certain is that the 'Open Door' experience has broadened the minds of Chinese businesspeople to new opportunities.

What Deng described as "Mind Liberation" was a sensitive and successful re-evaluation of Confucian values meshed with the challenge of global engagement, but on China's terms. The Open Door reforms perfectly complemented the entrepreneurial spirit of many ordinary Chinese, while reinforcing equal-result-oriented decision-making and the social ideals of communalism. Most importantly the reforms enabled the introduction of 'Capitalism with a Chinese face'. It was a case of China making a domestic political decision to choose the most appropriate aspects of the free market for the benefit of the greatest number of citizens — urbanites and farmers alike — not the free market dictating the terms to China. Deng Xiao Ping said that "socialism is not about poverty and poverty is not socialism, and to get rich is glorious" and "Black cat, white cat, what does it matter if it catches rats". For China it is the outcome, not the dogma or the rhetoric, that counts.

'Business Fever'

The turning point was marked by a movement against the traditional values that held *business to be unscrupulous*. More and more Chinese people now see a career in business as an acceptable, even desirable vocation. Initially this led to what the Chinese press called 'business fever', particularly between 1979 and 1997. At this time many Chinese people chose business as their best opportunity to make money. This situation was especially true of Chinese intellectuals who traditionally held the deepest contempt for business activities but now favoured business as one of the best career options. Many of them openly challenged the traditional value of 'study as a path to being an official'. This cultural shift has been the subject of a great deal of public interest, debate and research in China.

Business fever first emerged, or rather was identified, in 1984. At that time, many employees of state-owned enterprises, along with rural peasants, university students and even some intellectuals, began to enter the emerging part-time job market. The second 'outbreak', which occurred in 1990, was characterised by the defection of governmental officials and university lecturers to the commercial sector. Many thousands of China's best and brightest put aside the 'iron rice bowl' of state job security in favour of an uncertain future in the world of commerce.

Business fever had both immediate and long-term ramifications. In the short term, it meant a readjustment of salaries, conditions of employment and expectations, as China's experiment with 'Deng-style reforms' was tested for the first time. In the longer term, it meant a profound change in the traditional belief patterns of ordinary Chinese people and intellectuals. Business fever marked the beginning of the end of the cultural tradition that officialdom was the natural destination of a scholarly journey. In less than one generation, Chinese intellectuals had shifted from their position as the 'gatekeepers' of Confucian values to being some of China's greatest agents and advocates of social and economic change. This quickened the formulation and maturity of a modern business dynamic across the whole country. The reform policy has sent a clear and positive message to the educated and entrepreneurial class and has become a powerful motivator for engagement in commercial activities. Indeed, beyond the highest levels of government and bureaucracy, business is the most realistic means of achieving wealth. In this way the pursuit of riches is no longer openly condemned as a shameful activity, but rather encouraged as being in the best interests and development of the economy, and indeed the entire society. This modern Chinese business ethic can best be understood by examining the following key dimensions.

'Being rich is Glorious'

The new emphasis on equal opportunities, rather than equal results, represents a significant change of social values in China. Essentially, this has occurred since the early 1990s. Chinese society is complex, and as already explained, people in China have always been accustomed to inequality between the different social classes. Yet, paradoxically, it is a society where people of the same social rank have traditionally insisted on absolute equality. The concepts of 'result-equal orientation' and 'non self-pursuing wealth' have been deeply rooted in Chinese culture for thousands of years. Absolute, rather than relative equality among people of the same class, means priority has been given to equality in terms of income, rather than efficiency in competition. Recalling the words of Confucius, "don't worry that the people are poor, but rather be concerned if wealth is not equally allocated", it is easy to see why in the past people held a hostile attitude towards business and the accompanying competition for wealth. Significantly, this sentiment was inconsistent with one of the Deng's most important policies, namely to cautiously encourage the emergence of an affluent business class. It has become an accepted fact in some sections of society that individuals deserve 'glory' if they are succeeding, fairly, in commercial competition with equal opportunities.

In the past, Confucian values strongly suggested that the pursuit of profit was immoral (Feng, 1985). For obvious reasons this notion has been repudiated by an emerging generation of Chinese businesspeople and enterprise managers. Chinese businesspeople now argue that a profitable business is an efficient, equitable and realistic use of physical and human resources and that in this respect it is an acceptable expression of 'community'. Conversely, an unproductive or unprofitable business is now considered a waste of resources and deserves to be bankrupt. Consequently businesspeople now argue for the importance of their new role in ensuring the balance of society as a whole. This shift in the social evaluation of business has meant that most Chinese people today accept that good business means a stronger, more confident and prosperous nation.

China's economic reformers have sought to redress these older values by promulgating a number of popular mission-statement-like slogans such as "give priority to efficiency by giving consideration to equality". These words have become the rallying-cry of the emerging managerial class in China. People have now come to accept that efficiency equals profit, and that competition for profit leads to wealth and opportunity for the nation as a whole. This fundamental change in values has produced the belief that a commercial organisation deserves to fail if it cannot meet a number of basic expectations. As already mentioned, these include the notion that an enterprise must benefit the entire community; that a business must produce a profit; and that a particular firm must be competitive in the market. Clearly in a global economy, successful businesses must be competitive. Some Chinese now have a well-developed sense of competitive values. While in the past, many regarded these aspects of business as the 'shortcomings of capitalism', people's attitudes towards business nowadays have almost completely changed.

The impact of this new and positive evaluation of business activities on Chinese society as a whole has been profound. The social groups who have been able to adapt to and profit from these rapid social and economic changes feel both excited and encouraged. Equally, however, there are many who have not benefited from the transformations that have taken place and who still maintain the traditional value of 'equality in results'. The latter feel extremely frustrated, even outraged, at the ongoing reforms. Many of these groups simply cannot adjust to rapid social change, either technically or psychologically. The tension between promise and practice in the context of the reform process remains one of China's greatest challenges.

The Importance of Friendship

'Business succeeds on amicability' is a traditional value that has become a prominent feature of modern Chinese business culture. It emphasises friendly cooperation as the basis for success. Chinese businesspeople strongly believe that in business, friendships are more important than regulations or outcomes. They believe that harmony brings business opportunities, while anger or confrontation is likely to cause a loss of business. Confucianism emphasises the role of moral principles instead of legal regulations. For Chinese businesspeople 'good feelings' play a key role in the development and maintenance of good business. Under some circumstances, business will be conducted without a contract, as a friendship-building exercise. Many discussions, particularly with Chinese officials, are informal, non-contractual and friendly in nature. In China, foreigners are offered many opportunities to develop friendships. Later, they are also given an opportunity to reciprocate this kindness.

Chinese businesspeople will go to great lengths to end discussions on 'a friendly note'. There is a common expression, which says, "no deal this time, but friendship between two parties continues". Friendship is a prerequisite for achieving both business and personal goals. The deal itself can always be made at another time. Generally speaking modern-day Chinese businesspeople believe that commerce is not necessarily a case of 'winner takes all', but rather a discourse which results in wins for both sides.

Chinese businesspeople use the expression *tang sheng yi*, meaning 'talking business', whereas in the West, people tend to say 'doing business'. This is because Chinese businesspeople believe that it is through friendly discussions, often over the dinner table, that harmony and trust are established. People in China expect that this cooperative attitude will bring business prosperity. Equally, a failure to appreciate key social values will lead to the failure of any company in the Chinese market, whether foreign or local.

Another business practice related to the value of 'business succeeds on amicability' is the Chinese way of saying 'no' indirectly. Western businesspeople easily say 'no' to their counterparts when rejecting an offer or compromise. This is especially true if they think the offer is quite unacceptable. However, Chinese businesspeople will do everything they can to avoid saying 'no' directly, although they may not agree with the terms or conditions on offer. This should be seen in the context of 'business succeeds on amicability' and the desire to protect the 'face' of one's business partners and associates. Chinese businesspeople believe that directly saying 'no' to a partner or associate may engender hurt and therefore damage a valued friendship or 'network relationship', which in turn may lead to a loss of potential business in the long term. Chinese people generally believe that having to directly say 'no' embarrasses both parties. You will often hear the words "the matter is under consideration", graciously mentioned around the negotiating table. This expression is code to indicate, without offence, that your offer has been rejected or is incomplete. Chinese businesspeople will tell you that what is actually happening here is that your Chinese counterpart is protecting your 'face'. Many Western businesspeople insist that the Chinese side should tell them directly if they do not intend to accept an offer. Clearly, this is a matter of diametrically opposing cultural perceptions.

The reluctance to directly say 'no' is not only restricted to negotiations between counterparts, but also encompasses a wide range of relationships. Many Chinese maintain that it is better to say nothing than to say 'no', especially if they have to relay any sort of bad news. For instance, in China an unsuccessful applicant for employment will never receive notification that they have not been called to interview, whereas most Western companies have no trouble in providing this courtesy. This practice is reflected across the Chinese business world. A foreign businessperson should not be surprised or insulted when they don't receive a response to their inquiry. Other means have to be found of addressing the problem, such as discussing the matter over the table at the ubiquitous formal banquet, or by using a formal gift presentation to make subtle enquires, or by third party representations.

Guanxi

Personal relationships play a pre-eminent role in Chinese commerce and Chinese businesspeople pay a lot of attention to the establishment of extensive personal friendship networks. Because of the influence of the twin values of 'high uncertainty avoidance' and 'face', Chinese businesspeople strongly believe that networking is one of the keys to increase security for business success. Traditionally, people were expected to follow the rules of senior people, ancestors, or Heaven, in order to reduce personal and social uncertainty. Nowadays, businesspeople believe that establishing a strong and extensive *guanxi*-network can reduce risks and competition.

In the *guanxi*-network, businesspeople can advance their interests by dealing with people who are trustworthy and able to protect each other in business. Confucianism argues that if people learnt to trust each other more, laws and regulations would be practically unnecessary. It also advocates that people in a *guanxi*-network should reciprocate in terms of showing each other 'face'. They should also be ready to help other members of the network in business and can expect their assistance to be repaid in kind. This reciprocity even extends to what might be considered an unreasonable request, such as conducting some illegal business deal.

There are several practical reasons for these kinds of arrangements. First, competition is fierce and certain resources are limited in China. This includes a permanent shortage of raw materials for production, as well as limited intangible resources such as access to capital or permission to trade (although the situation is no where near as bad as it was in the 1980s). Almost all businesses in China must hold a specific license. These permits are issued by a number of central or local governmental authorities as a means of rationing limited resources. At any given time, there are many applicants waiting for permission to use these resources and your success in obtaining a permit will depend very much on you having a good relationship with the relevant government department. Suppliers and officials must follow the regulations that govern these applications, but often an official is at liberty to assist a member of his or her network group in a particular matter by 'fast-tracking' applications. With China's entry into the WTO, this type of competition will be reduced by more openness and accountability in the bureaucratic system.

Second, a centralised economy tends to result in only a few empowered individuals making important decisions or binding agreements. The hierarchical values of Chinese culture supports a less than democratic style of decision making in most Chinese organisations. Having a special *guanxi* relationship with the people in charge is a necessary fact of business life. It is crucial to identify and quickly establish good relations with these key people. For example, a marketer will have a great deal of difficulty placing his or her goods on display in a prominent and successful CBD retail outlet, if he or she is unable to establish a business relationship with a key person within the particular department store. The more significant the business is, the more crucial the *guanxi* may be. *Guanxi is* recognised as a crucial strategy to compete in the Chinese market (Luo, 1997*). Guanxi* with buyers, suppliers, transportation staff, in fact anyone related to the business at hand, is considered important and worth nurturing.

Guanxi is also believed to help secure real business success. While it is true that people use *guanxi* with the intention of establishing and strengthening long term commercial relationships, the key point is that *guanxi* is based on more than trust. A combination of trust and utility forms the basis of process and outcome. Likewise reciprocal purpose, or the perception that both parties are willing and able to return favours in the future, is a crucial component of *guanxi*. This last point is a necessary element for effectiveness in any business network.

For the Chinese these *guanxi* relationships hold a value that is superior to money. Chinese businesspeople regard business relationship networks as a commercial investment, or rather as a form of insurance. In the West, and especially in the United States, a much-loved phrase is 'time is money'. Westerners easily infer that the Chinese have a different concept of time and are not concerned with time as a commercially measurable asset. Rather, it is believed that the Chinese spend too much time in the service of relationships (Fatehi, 1996). Actually, Chinese businesspeople accept that time is money, but look at it from a different perspective. Their logic is that time spent on relationships will effectively generate money by creating a favourable climate in which business activities may take place. In their view, time spent on hard work *per se*, with no relationship, is ultimately a waste of time. This is the main reason why Chinese businesspeople hold so many formal banquets and lavish expensive gifts on guests or dignitaries. They are investing in their business future. It is often found that a Chinese firm will allocate a seemingly disproportionate amount of their budget and energy to the nurturing of 'important friendships'. This is also why most prospective Chinese joint venture partners go to so much trouble to explain to their foreign counterparts the extent of their influence within a network, especially in respect to the bureaucracy. Currently, some foreign companies or joint ventures in China also employ this approach in their business practice.

The relationship network is usually based on the intuitive qualities of personal feelings. If a foreign businessperson has not established a relationship with crucial persons or with the appropriate government departments, then their experience in China will be a frustrating one. They will almost certainly encounter innumerable obstacles. And in the end they will fail. However Chinese businesspeople will commit themselves wholeheartedly to a project if they feel that there is friendship and trust between parties.

Case Study: Promotion or *Guanxi*?

One firm based in Auckland, New Zealand, a health care product manufacturing company hoping to set up business in China, had difficulty finding distributors. They advertised extensively across China in both newspapers and magazines. There was no response whatsoever. The firm then tried a different strategy. They sent sales agents to various Chinese cities to promote their product. This considerable effort also failed. The cost of in-country operations and advertising by this time was extremely high. The company was faced with the decision to withdraw from the Chinese market. On the advice of a business culture consultant based in Beijing, it became convinced that a complete lack of *guanxi* was the cause of their failure. The same consultant introduced key figures from the New Zealand group to someone within her own *guanxi* network, an official in charge of a division in the Department of Commerce in Beijing. This official was also hired as a consultant. The New Zealanders were soon working co-operatively with a local businessperson who controlled a mature distribution network. The firm's products were immediately placed in the market and it later estimated that the cost spent on establishing *guanxi* was approximately one fiftieth the previous combined expenses of advertising and promotion, but with a much better outcome.

As this case study shows, *guanxi* has real commercial value. To exploit the advantages of network relationships in China is however a delicate challenge for foreign businesspeople. Most successful foreign companies in China use the expert services of consultants who specialise in reducing the risk associated with cultural misunderstandings that often occur in the initial building phase of *guanxi*. This is because both sides must not only build trust, but be also be convinced that the relationship has long term positive commercial benefits.

The 'Seamlessness' of Business and Officialdom

Although traditional Chinese values perceive commerce and trade in a negative light in pre-modern, traditional China, business activities were still essential to the life of the nation. There are many examples of various Chinese government's attempting to control national commerce and trade in order to impose stability. There is an unbroken philosophy of government which ensured that state officials controlled business. The objective of this state intervention was to limit business's alleged socially destabilising influence. Naturally governmental officials themselves became involved in commerce, using their privileged positions to guarantee business success. Gradually, many came to accept that a 'seamless' relationship between business and bureaucracy was a successful way to conduct commerce.

Throughout the history of China, many governments have

reinforced the value of a seamless relationship between business and bureaucracy through their trade policies. The Qing Government, for instance, in enacting a closed door trade policy from 1757 onwards, dictated that only a select few officials should be involved in operating China's commercial relationships with the outside world and that this trade should be conducted out of one location, namely Guangzhou City (Canton). These officials represented the Qing Government in all aspects of international trade. This established powerful monopolies across the entire spectrum of international trade.

Likewise, after the Communist Party of China assumed office in 1949, foreign trade still came under the control of government. Ordinary enterprises were deemed to have no right to engage in international commerce. Only a select few governmental companies were permitted to engage in foreign trade. These Chinese companies specialised in the purchase of domestically produced agricultural and industrial products. They then traded these products against foreign goods and services on the open market. In a sense it was back to the 'bad old days' of the Qing Dynasty, when only a few governmental officials were permitted to deal directly with foreigners. This situation remained virtually unchanged until 1978.

Authorising qualified companies to enter in foreign trade negotiations was an important aspect of China's economic reform package. Currently, many large, state-owned organisations, corporations, private companies and joint ventures have the right to deal with foreign companies. The culturally sanctioned privilege of a few governmental companies, who until recently monopolised China's foreign trade, has been broken. Unfortunately the notion of a seamless relationship between business and bureaucracy still influences the realities of today's business culture. Most Chinese people take it for granted that a successful business must have a close relationship with individual government officials. This entrenched viewpoint partially explains the historical and cultural background to the widespread corruption that exists in China today. How culture interfaces with business in the context of a strong state system will be the subject of Chapter Six.

Arising out of the 'seamlessness' of business and officialdom, the official seal is a unique phenomenon in Chinese business. Whereas in the West, contracts and documents are confirmed by an individual signature, in China contracts, or important letters, must be stamped with the company's seal or that of a relevant government department. Chinese businesspeople generally think that the company seal is more credible than a personal signature. If a high-level document has a signature, but not a company seal, then its value and credibility are questioned. This is further evidence that Chinese people have a group orientation, which emphasises collective rather than individual responsibility. The organisational stamp or company seal represents a formal type of collective responsibility for agreements contracted in the documents.

Any individual signature, even that of the top manager, cannot represent an entire organisation, hence, the importance of a signature is limited. In China, contracts are only considered valid if seals are affixed to both sides of the document. Foreign businesspersons must pay very careful attention to this. This vital information could effectively protect your interests in the case of a legal dispute. One final point on this matter: a valid document may require the affixing of quite a number of official seals. Due to the bureaucratic nature of the Chinese government, the affixing of seals often takes time. Chinese businesspeople make a joke of this long procedure by referring to it as 'official seal travelling'. In this respect, the fixing of seals should be considered as much ceremonial as legal.

Good Fortune in Business

As mentioned, Confucianism proposes that Heaven influences and assists people in their daily lives and careers. For many Chinese individuals, believing in Heaven also means believing in fate, or rather fortune. A common Chinese saying is 'people make plans but their successful implementation depends on Heaven'. This belief does not abrogate initiative. Rather, it means that while a good plan depends on personal ability, ultimately success may be determined by factors that are sometimes beyond a person's control. These factors belong to the realm of the supernatural. The Chinese call this 'the willingness of Heaven'. Accordingly, Chinese business-people put great stock in *feng shui*, which can roughly be translated as atmosphere and orientation, lucky numbers, and visage. These factors are all believed to influence fate and fortune in commerce.

Feng shui is an ancient system of mystical knowledge, which claims to be able to look into the future by examining the physical orientation of an environment. Followers of *feng shui* believe that there is a sympathetic relationship between the earth and the rest of the cosmos and that positive or negative influences are present in every physical location. During the Cultural Revolution, fortune, good luck and *feng shui* were denounced as feudal remnants. However, the Chinese government now takes a more tolerant attitude towards a variety of religious beliefs or superstitions, including *feng shui*. The traditional values of good fortune and *feng shui* have gradually recovered their prominence in China. It is interesting that many overseas Chinese businesspeople are also strongly influenced by certain aspects of traditional Chinese culture, including a fascination with the notion of good fortune, especially in as far as it relates to their commercial activities. This in turn has influenced, or as some people unkindly suggest, re-infected, mainland China. Dong Jian-Huai, the Chief Executive of the Hong Kong Special Administrative Region, (SAR) for instance, asked a *feng shui* master to identify the best place for his new office. This is an indication of the respectability that *feng shui* still holds. Currently in China, *feng shui* is a common practice in commercial activities and business decisions. Businesspeople will ask a *feng shui* master to identify the orientation and location of buildings before deciding whether to invest in real estate or select a business office, because good *feng shui* means good fortune.

'Lucky numbers' are now again the most popular means of determining good fortune amongst Chinese businesspeople. As in the West, the number 13 is believed to be unlucky. The Chinese consider the number 4 to be unlucky because it sounds like the Chinese word for death. On the other hand, the numbers 6, 8 and 9 are thought to bring good luck, The 8th day of the 8th month of 1988 was in fact considered by many Chinese to be the luckiest day in human history. Many couples took advantage of this lucky day to get married. The number 8 is actually considered to mean prosperity.

The number 6 represents a smooth life without trouble. The sound of the number *9* is like the Chinese expression for 'a long time', so this number is interpreted as *continuous* growth without failure. Chinese businesspeople are always trying to choose these numbers and avoid the unlucky ones in their private and business lives. They will pay a high premium for 'lucky' telephone numbers or car registration plates. Indeed, registered phone numbers or car licence plates are sold by public auction in some Chinese cities — the telephone number 87888 recently went for 129,000 RMB yuan (about $US15,998) at an auction in Hangchou in Zhejiang Province.

The Chinese preoccupation with numbers affects almost every aspect of business practice. A date based on lucky numbers must be chosen for the launch of a new company. In an office block, the floor level must coincide with an appropriate lucky number, with higher prices being offered for floor numbers 6, 8 and 9. This is particularly true of prices for apartments in the Beijing CBD. People do not like to stay in level 13 in most Chinese office buildings. Likewise, room 13s in hotels or office buildings are disliked. The fascination with good fortune even goes so far as being a determinant of price. Many luxury goods are priced by lucky numbers in order to attract customers. Even the date of advertising must be chosen according to a date that corresponds with a lucky number.

Finally, judging a person by their visage or countenance — that is, their facial features and expressions — is another ancient practice still commonly employed by many Chinese businesspeople. It is believed that kindness or treachery can be discerned through the observation of a person's physiognomy and special precautions are will be taken in respect of someone whose appearance is thought to be negative or unlucky.

Stratagems in Business

The modern Chinese businessperson believes that commerce is warfare by other means, and that the commercial field is really a field of battle. To win commercial battles is a serious pursuit and like a military commander, Chinese businesspeople will employ recognised tactics when negotiating deals, building *guanxi*, or developing strategies for international competition. The way that Chinese businesspeople deal with this situation is by drawing on their vast historical experience of domestic warfare. They apply stratagems and tactics that were developed over a period of over 2000 years.

Chinese business strategies are far reaching. Chinese business is an international exercise because Chinese capital is a global phenomenon. Outposts of Chinese influence and mercantile wealth radiate from 'Mother China' like the spokes of a wheel: Vancouver, San Francisco, Sydney, Surabaya, Semarang, Singapore, Kuala Lumpur and Hong Kong form a chain of Pacific-rim sources of Chinese power that strategically place China at their cultural and economic epicentre. It is through these far-flung 'branch offices' that Chinese business has invested huge amounts of capital in the international market, while at the same time luring foreign companies and investment houses into China-based joint ventures.

For instance, in September 1996 the United States Ministry of Finance announced that the Chinese government and some Chinese companies controlled by the Chinese government, had to date purchased some US$12.1 billion in American Treasury bonds. This trend continues and is consistent with the strategic outlook of Chinese business, where the aim is to take the battle into the enemy's territory. Due to China's involvement in the global economy, many Chinese businesspeople believe that to be successful in a competitive international environment one must first be an excellent strategist. They suppose that one must not only possess professional knowledge, but also imagination, wisdom, skill and strategy.

Chinese culture bristles with treatises describing strategies, skills and tactics for gaining the advantage in a wide range of 'battlefield situations', both real and metaphorical. One of the best known is Sun Zi's (Sun Tzu's) 'Thirty-six Stratagems'. The author of this document was the most successful general in ancient Chinese history.

General Sun Zi's work is widely read by both Chinese and foreign businesspeople and is considered as relevant today as it was when it was written in the fifth century B.C.

Eight Examples of the Thirty-six Stratagems of Sun Zi

1. Make use of camouflage. Weaken your enemy's position by concealing your own machinations.
2. Be patient. Let your enemies make mistakes and become divided, then attack them aggressively while they are retreating.
3. Be patient. Induce your enemies to use up their resources. Provoke them but do not attack until you have a clear advantage.
4. Put up a false front. Mislead or bluff your adversaries. Attack when your enemy is confused.
5. Reveal only one strategy to your adversary at a time but have a secret plan that will catch them off guard and give you an advantage.
6. When there is dissension in the ranks of your enemy, be patient. Allow them time to become even weaker, then attack.
7. Find out everything possible about an adversary before taking any action. Then act quickly and decisively.
8. Use various ruses to get your adversary into your territory on your terms.

Chapter 4

Chinese Negotiating Style

This chapter explains the rules of the Chinese negotiating 'game'. This contest involves new skills that must be learned, practised and then applied. Negotiations in China involve a complex combination of economic transactions, negotiating philosophy, protocol, and practice. This chapter describes in detail the composition, tactics, motives and strategies that have made the Chinese so successful in business since 1978. The managerial system and hierarchical values of many Chinese organisations is explained, as are the roles of the various members of the negotiating team. Understanding the characteristics of Chinese negotiating strategy and appreciating the specific role, function and concerns of each person within the negotiating framework, is an effective means of speeding up the negotiating process and ensuring a mutually satisfactory agreement. In addition the role of relationship-building leisure activities, such as evening banquets, receptions and ceremonies, attending cultural performances or even sightseeing is outlined. One of the key recommendations is for foreign businesspeople to learn how to adapt individual strategies to complement, not clash, with the Chinese style of negotiating. This includes being aware that the negotiation process is completely open-ended and not constrained by agreements, or even contracts. There is also important and practical information on the role and function of the Chinese banquet, and how various forms of hospitality can be used as powerful tools for relationship-building in business.

Negotiation is a crucial aspect of any business culture. It is a contest, and potentially it can involve cultural conflict, especially if the negotiating parties have little or no appreciation of each other's style. There are many books and journal articles available which offer Western readers general knowledge about negotiating skills in the context of Chinese business culture. However, these books often serve up information as understanding, which is not always the case.

The Rules of Negotiation

It has been argued that cross-culture negotiations contain all of the complexity of normal negotiations, with the added dimensions of cultural diversity (Adler, 1997). Negotiation between Westerners and Chinese typically involves complicated cross-cultural issues, incorporating both economic transactions and cultural activities (Fang, 1999). The fundamental difference between Chinese and Western negotiating protocol is that the Chinese emphasise both hierarchical rank and 'face protection', while Westerners stress business efficiency and contractual process. The Chinese like to maintain a tight hierarchical control over the entire negotiating process. These cultural traits format the Chinese negotiating style in respect to the composition of the team, the roles of members within the negotiating group, the means of negotiating and the way of implementing results. Some Western businesspeople claim that the negotiating process in Chinese business is too complex to be comprehensively understood. While it may be complex, it is actually very predictable.

The Initial Stage: Roles and Relationships

Differentiating Roles
The Chinese prefer to use a large negotiating team, especially

when dealing with foreigners. Teams usually include technical members and administrators, but sometimes involve representatives of local, provincial or national authorities, especially if negotiations take place overseas. These officials may be included in negotiations because of their position within the hierarchy, or because their views may have some bearing on the final decision. Alternatively, these officials may simply be taking advantage of the opportunity to travel overseas and may appear not to make any sort of contribution whatsoever.

The managerial system and hierarchical values of many Chinese organisations determine that people play the role of the negotiator and decision-maker for different reasons at different times. To effectively deal with a Chinese negotiating group it is important to identify the team's various members. For example, a Chinese delegation representing a state-owned organisation is often composed of two parts. One part includes technicians or professionals who are responsible for collecting technical information. These people provide the team with an assessment of the significance and feasibility of the other sides offer. Chinese technical negotiators will take an active part in actual discussions. They freely and easily communicate but have no authority to make substantive decisions. In the final analysis they merely summit their findings to the person or persons at the top of the negotiating hierarchy for consideration.

The second part of a typical state-owned organisation negotiating team is made up of representatives of commercial and other bureaucratic departments. These officials are responsible for handling prices and shipments, as well as other high level issues such as equity and capital injection. This second group is considered to be the Chinese team's 'tough negotiators'.

However, the 'real' decision-makers, the person or persons who make the final decision on behalf of the Chinese side, may not appear at the negotiating table at all. They may be above and separate to the two parts of the active negotiating team. This 'super group' waits for negotiators to complete their assessment and then takes time to study the information, subsequently raising and preparing questions for a second round of talks. This super group remotely controls the entire process.

In some instances, the real decision-maker may be a member of the second part of the Chinese negotiating group. He or she will usually sit silently and appear to contribute nothing towards the joint meeting. This is because Chinese hierarchical values mean that very senior managers should not be physically active in negotiations but utilise their strategic intellect. Such an individual enjoys immense power behind the scenes.

Senior Chinese managers argue that receiving reports from subordinates, not only strengthens their position, but also benefits the negotiating process by obtaining time for reflection. The demarcated roles of negotiators and decision-makers in a Chinese-style negotiating situation usually means that the final decision takes longer than it would in the West. Often this is interpreted as a delaying tactic. This leads to frustration and resentment, especially on the part of the leader of a negotiating team from a Western company where individualism and personal responsibility are highlighted. For example, a senior executive in a Western firm may like to present him or herself as a person of authority, capable of making a decision on the spot.

Understanding the characteristics of Chinese negotiating strategies and appreciating the specific role, function and concerns of each person within the negotiating framework is an effective means of speeding up this process and ensuring a mutually satisfactory agreement. Being aware that an inefficient bureaucracy sometimes causes a deferment of the final decision also helps to explain delays.

The first challenge is to identify the actual decision-maker and gain direct access to him or her. This is a matter of determining just *who is who*. There are four ways to do this.

- You can exchange a written list of members of both negotiating teams before the first joint meeting. Examining your Chinese counterparts' positions or formal titles on this list will indicate each team member's role. Often, Chinese people record their names in hierarchical order, with the name at the top being that of the most important person in the hierarchy.

- The order of formal introductions at the beginning of deliberations may also indicate the relative rank of Chinese negotiators. Normally the Chinese like to arrange for an interpreter, or an individual of lower rank, to introduce team members, working downward from the highest to the lowest ranked position. The person first introduced is always the most powerful member of the team.

- Foreign businesspeople should also observe the seating position of their Chinese counterparts around the negotiating or banquet table. This will augment the intelligence you have already gathered, by either confirming or calling into question the relative position of each player. Typically, the most senior Chinese negotiators will sit at the centre of the negotiating table, with their assistants placed on either side in descending order or rank.

- Scrutinising personal name cards is another means of determining who are the key negotiators. Business cards will differentiate managers from technical people by title and qualifications. Any senior manager should be treated cautiously — he or she may or may not be the decision-maker. Initially, it is wise to regard all managers as decision-makers, especially if their roles can not be clearly identified by other means.

One important thing to note in the composition of the respective negotiating teams is that the titles and position of members of the foreign negotiating side should at least match, or be of a higher standing, than those of the Chinese team. The more senior the standing of members on the foreigners' team, the more the Chinese team will believe that their counterparts take them and their offer of business seriously.

The Chinese manner of negotiation is both prescriptive and predictable. As indicated, many Westerners unwisely claim that the process of negotiation in a Chinese context is inscrutable. As this chapter will demonstrate, while Chinese negotiation style is complex, it is also highly predictable, even scripted.

The Foundation Stone: Interpersonal Relationships

Rather than launch immediately into direct business discussions, Chinese negotiators will first wish to talk with their counterparts about a whole range of non-business related subjects. This may include broad and convivial discussions about culture, art, history or food customs, but will usually also involve friendly questions about social or personal life. The purpose of this is to judge whether an interpersonal relationship can be established between counterparts prior to negotiations. Chinese businesspeople have a great desire to demonstrate their respect for counterparts as a means of establishing mutual credibility. This is a genuine attempt at establishing a friendship relationship, but at the same time it is also a strategy to maximise opportunities and to ensure the success of negotiations. Notwithstanding the fact that all businesspeople are ultimately capable of breaking a promise or changing contracts, the Chinese believe that a strong personal relationship cannot easily be ruined or broken.

A personal relationship is considered to be absolutely necessary for good business practice. It is considered more reliable than contracts or law, in that it guarantees the social and moral commitment of both sides to achieve a negotiated goal. According to Chinese business perceptions, there will always be unpredictable or difficult issues to solve during and after formal negotiations. The Chinese believe that the best way to deal with this is to secure a sincere commitment from both sides to work together. They believe that commitment is based on trust, and trust is built on firm relationships. The experience of domestic Chinese business reinforces this practice. Consequently, the Chinese prefer to start with informal non-business discussions that hopefully lead to the establishment of friendships prior to the beginning of negotiations. Negotiators will make every effort to build up personal relationships from the very beginning of the negotiating process. These efforts often take the form of a variety of leisure activities such as evening banquets, receptions and ceremonies, attending cultural performances or even sightseeing.

For Western business negotiators, the initial stage of personal relationship building, which may include participation in a wide range of social and cultural activities, can appear to be a complete waste of time, money and energy. According to many Westerners, this often-convoluted ritual is too much to bear. Consequently, frustrated foreigners frequently seek to rush through outstanding issues in the vain hope that this will speed up a negotiated settlement. This invariably proves to be an incorrect assumption.

Many Westerners are particularly task and efficiency-oriented and often see little need to attend to non-task related topics in conversation with their Chinese counterpart — they usually want to come straight to the point. The individualist nature and formality of many Western legal systems supports this business practice. However, if negotiations are to be successful, then task-orientated individuals will have to look at the benefits of adapting their strategy to complement, not clash, with the Chinese style of negotiating.

The Middle Stage: Patience and Compromise

In general, there is a definite advantage in learning as much as possible about cross-cultural ways of doing things. As suggested, by playing by the rules, Westerners can even beat the Chinese at their own game. By anticipating the next step in the process, Westerners can pre-empt certain culturally-motivated moves. Because Westerners are outside the Chinese cultural paradigm, they are able to develop an outside-in view that will put negotiations into an objective, rather than subjective, cultural perspective. They can step back and with skill and confidence, control the situation in the same way as the Chinese decision-makers normally do. This will ultimately speed up the entire process and prevent either side from seeking out a competitor because of misunderstanding or frustration.

Patience

When negotiations become more focused, the Chinese technological negotiators are often found to act as messengers.

They collect information but resist making statements about possible deals. They try and learn as much as possible about the other side's goals, advantages, disadvantages and interests. They then faithfully report this information back to the real decision-makers within their organisation. In subsequent rounds of discussions the Chinese team will negotiate according to the remote instructions of the decision-makers. Each time the negotiating teams meet, the process will be repeated again as more information is collected for further reports and the negotiations as a whole may often involve several rounds of talks. The purpose of this is to establish at the outset an in-principle agreement about common goals. Discussions can then gradually become more detailed as various specifics are introduced into the forum for debate.

This approach arises from Chinese cultural values, the carefully defined role of negotiators, the hierarchical managerial system, and even tactical or strategic concerns. Chinese businesspeople like to digest information before they contemplate a decision. They then prefer to step back from the process and think over offers or speculate about perceived traps. This avoids uncertainty, as negotiations become more critical. In turn everything must be reported back to higher management and often to different departments or levels of administration. This maintains hierarchical power in the form of a collective responsibility for the final decision.

For foreign businesspeople operating in China it is important to practice patience. Because of hierarchical social values, the peculiarities of the Chinese managerial system, a desire to develop friendships, as well as tactical concerns, Chinese negotiators will often prolong the negotiating process. Conversely, their foreign counterparts will usually wish to reduce time-consuming activities where possible. However, they should be careful in this matter. Their Chinese counterparts may take advantage of their impatience, especially if the foreign negotiators have indicated anxiety about signing the contract because of time restraints or expense. Remember the stratagems of General Sun Tsu. Foreign counterparts must be prepared to negotiate longer than they might expect. Meanwhile, they can look for a reasonable excuse to justify a truncation of the negotiating time.

Compromise

Unlike other Asian negotiators, such as Koreans or Japanese who strongly resist offering concessions during negotiations, Chinese negotiators like to bargain. They see the offering of concessions at any time during negotiations as prudent practice. This is true of both private business and government-owned enterprises. Chinese businesspeople see the offering of concessions as an important component of the overall process.

Negotiating objectives can be prioritised as follows: what must achieved; what is hoped to be achieved; and what is considered a desirable outcome. Simultaneously, negotiators will constantly relate concessions to objectives in terms of what is to be conceded. The process is further divided into two hypothetical positions. The first is, 'What constitutes a modest concession?' And second, 'What concession is the negotiating team least willing to concede?' When a negotiator uses a most-willing-to-concede concession to gain an objective, this is regarded by the Chinese side as a 'win' in the negotiations.

For many Western negotiators, compromise is generally regarded as a half-win, half-lose failure, rather than an outright 'win-win' solution. This is because Westerners generally set the negotiable point too close to the bottom line at the beginning of the process. Chinese negotiators, however, generally use compromise as a major device, regarding it as an opportunity to manoeuvre towards a win-win solution. The Chinese will provide counterparts with a 'most willing to concede' concession at the negotiating table in the very beginning of the process, holding back other more delicate concessions. The latter will subsequently be offered as required. In other words, Chinese negotiators will typically leave plenty of room for compromise within a possible range of settlement options. One must bargain first and then look for an agreement. The Chinese consider a counterpart who is not willing to bargain as less than genuinely interested in doing a deal, especially if there are few or no compromises offered along the way. Western negotiators who offer few or no compromises are considered by their Chinese counterparts as inflexible or insincere. The most effective way of dealing with Chinese negotiators is to leave enough room for compromise at the beginning of the negotiating process and then proceed to an agreement by offering concessions.

Tactics to avoid

Inevitably there will be disagreement between sides during most negotiations. The question is how to reach an agreement without losing substantial interests, or jeopardising the entire process? There are many ways of addressing this problem. A Western negotiator may use whatever skills and strategies are available to handle disputes or disagreements. There is, however, one strategy, common in the West, which must not be used and this is to 'push' negotiations by exerting power or position to the extent that it will injure a Chinese counterpart's 'face'. No matter how attractive a deal may be to them, many Chinese negotiators and decision-makers will terminate discussions if they feel that their 'face' has been hurt.

There are three main reasons why Chinese negotiators may suddenly call a premature end to discussions. As already indicated, many Chinese people are sensitive about their public image due to the high premium placed on 'face protection'. A 'loss of face' may extend beyond potential or perceived affronts to their person, to include slights to their company or to their nation. Chinese people like to be respected and they are proud of the ancient history, as well as contemporary success and achievements of their country. They insist on fair treatment in terms of their position within the hierarchy and will not easily tolerate being 'looked down on'. This exists to the extent that under certain circumstances Chinese people see 'face protection' as more important than 'good business'.

Another reason is that because Chinese business culture is strongly influenced by the traditional value of collectivism, most Chinese are concerned about their relationship with others and with other people's feelings towards them. Forms of behaviour should be reciprocal between persons of a similar social standing and courtesies extended to others are expected to be returned in a like manner. This expectation, however, is not always realised in intercultural business practice. Because of advances in Western technology, management practice and even legal systems, some foreign businesspeople feel superior to their Chinese negotiating counterparts. Additionally, foreigners who are influenced by individualist values, often take action based on their position, interests and feelings without considering the impact on others. As a result, many Western businesspeople have little regard for Chinese customs or concerns. Many feel that cultural differences are either unimportant or don't exist at all. For this reason they place a dangerously low premium on understanding cultural diversity. This attitude might be interpreted as 'looking down' on their Chinese partners at the negotiating table, presenting what the Chinese may identify as 'a superior air'. It would hurt the negotiation process if such a manner was accidentally presented on one occasion but if such an attitude were to dominate the proceedings, then the game might be over before it actually started. This is especially true if Chinese negotiators find that their foreign counterparts appear to be repeatedly ignoring their concerns.

Finally, some Chinese negotiators, or key decision-makers, are representatives of state-owned or collective enterprises or companies. The personnel management characteristics of these organisations ensures that issues of position and promotion are not always directly related to performance, but rather to relative seniority within the internal hierarchy of a particular organisation (although like everywhere employees who perform well are generally treated favourably). In this respect, negotiators may easily abandon a good deal if they feel insulted, as they believe that a successful outcome may not improve their relative standing with superiors or make a difference to their personal career. Alternatively, they may feel that a successful outcome would be too difficult to achieve and cease negotiations for the same reasons.

It is wise for foreign businesspeople to take a great deal of trouble to nurture a sense of mutual respect through the establishment of sound personal friendships with Chinese negotiators and other relevant people. Ultimately this will avoid disappointment, a sudden secession from discussions or substantive loss in the process of coming to a mutually satisfactory conclusion.

The Final Stage: The Win-Win Ending

Win-Win Orientation

There is no final stage in the Chinese negotiating process, even after the signing of an agreement. This is at odds with the situation in the West where negotiations are marked by a discrete beginning and culminate in a non-negotiable contract. Chinese businesspeople like to negotiate contracts that offer reasonable benefit for both sides. Many Chinese businesspeople believe that no one likes to participate in a business which causes anyone to lose 'face' and which does not ensure benefit for all participants (unlike the Japanese who often aim for the best possible position irrespective of their counterparts' loss). For the Chinese, an ideal result is that neither side is seen as 'the big loser'. Both sides must feel that negotiations have been fair and that the relationship will ultimately lead to solid business. Serious misunderstandings can occur after the so-called 'final stage' of the negotiation process. This is because Chinese negotiators consider the process to be completely open-ended. Many Western businesspeople complain that their Chinese counterparts continue to raise issues for further negotiation after an agreement has been signed.

The Potential for Frustration

For Western people, signing a contract means that both sides have agreed to cooperate on fixed conditions that have only to be implemented. For Chinese people, the signed agreement merely marks the end of the initial stage of cooperation. Subsequent cooperation is contingent on the condition that supplementary negotiations may be required before, during, or after implementation of an open-ended series of decisions. Chinese businesspeople argue that there is no such thing as a contract without loopholes and there will always be problems that cannot be anticipated at the time of initial negotiations. This is seen as being especially true for complicated or large-scale projects.

Chinese negotiators, being only too aware that the economic situation in China might lead to a failure of project cooperation with their Western counterparts, naturally want to reduce this risk through supplementary negotiations after signing the contract. Subsequently, both Chinese negotiators and their foreign counterparts are becoming more flexible in respect to the cultural requirements of China's changing economic environment.

Another factor that helps explain the problem of supplementary negotiations is that some Chinese businesspeople do not have a strong sense of the strict legal effectiveness of a contract or agreement. Many Chinese believe that the main features of an agreement or contract must be observed, but lesser points can be subject to change, depending on the depth of trust and the spirit of friendly cooperation between the parties involved. Chinese businesspeople normally keep their word in respect to implementing a contract. However, they will continue to seek 'sub-concessions' or 'interpretations' on specific points. This is seen as a means of securing more, not less, commitment to the stated goals of the agreement. This is not the way that many Western businesspeople see the situation.

Some Chinese businesspeople divide final negotiations into two phases: signing an intensive agreement and then agreeing to a contract. They believe that an agreement is less legally binding than a contract and that it only implies a basic intention to cooperate. According to their understanding, an agreement is subject to change in later bargaining. Hence Chinese businesspeople will sign an agreement in the first instance without hard bargaining. They will then use this as a foundation to construct a tough bargaining strategy that ultimately leads to the signing of a contract. Western businesspeople, however, regard an agreement as a legal document which, like a contract, is subject to fixed conditions.

This ambiguity is very frustrating for foreign negotiators. To reduce the potential for dispute, foreign negotiators are advised to work with their Chinese counterparts in carefully identifying the items within the contract that are beyond reasonable dispute. It is also necessary to explain thoroughly and then reaffirm with the Chinese negotiators the exact nature of an agreement or contract before signing it. This takes patience and is most effective if based on amicable relationships. Sometimes foreign negotiators may actually build into the agreement a mechanism for handling supplementary negotiations. In this way no one will be shocked or surprised when negotiations continue beyond the signing of a contract.

Termination with Opportunities Open

According to the Chinese, an experienced negotiator will avoid assuming a confrontational stance as this will threaten the success of present or future negotiations. Compared with Western negotiators, the Chinese use a less aggressive negotiating style. This is not to say that Chinese negotiators are less goal-oriented than their Western counterparts. The contrast arises from the Chinese desire for business success to be based on amicability and 'face protection'. An open dispute during negotiations is a danger signal; rather a sense of harmony is believed to the foundation stone of good business. Chinese businesspeople believe that harmony is contingent to the protection of one's 'face' and that aggressive behaviour in a public arena will hurt the 'face' of both parties. Invariably this public 'loss of face' will result in both personal and professional damage. Consequently, Chinese negotiators avoid the use of 'bitter' or strong words even though they may be unhappy or upset about the substance or outcome of deliberations and indeed may intend to terminate the meeting.

Chinese businesspeople will avoid, practically at all costs, being involved in court proceedings or public arbitration. If this has to happen, no matter what judgement results, they will feel that the Chinese principle of 'no deal this time, but friendship is still important', has been betrayed and that their organisation's public 'loss of face' will reflect poorly on their own negotiating prowess. According to the Chinese, public confrontation announces that the cooperative relationship between parties, based on trust and good feelings is over. This is the last thing anyone wants to see in a Chinese business relationship. By the time negotiations begin to breakdown a great deal of time, effort and money has been invested in both friendship building and networking. In their mind, open dispute creates a negative profile for both parties and calls into question their capacity to cooperate with anyone, let alone each other. This in turn casts a shadow over both parties' authority in the business community and can exert a sustained negative influence over their business with other companies or enterprises. An open dispute may ultimately lead to many lost opportunities.

The astute foreign businessperson can ensure the long-term success of their venture by adopting the Chinese style of negotiation. This is an investment not just in the job at hand, but also in profile and reputation. If negotiations have to be concluded prematurely, then both parties should take the opportunity to diplomatically suggest that the cessation is temporary. Frustrated Western businesspeople should avoid laying the blame on their Chinese counterparts or describing the negotiations as a failure. They should instead try to make the cancellation of dialogue smooth, positive and open-ended.

The Role of Banquets

In China, business is always related to eating. Practically every foreign businessperson that has ever visited China has received frequent invitations to a formal banquet. For most Westerners their lasting impression of China is the variety, abundance and taste of delicious food. There are many forms of banquets in China: a welcoming banquet, personal banquets, official banquets, company banquets, and farewell banquets. Treating foreigners to a variety of generous banquets in China is sometimes interpreted by foreign businesspeople as a Chinese business tactic to 'soften-up' their foreign counterparts by making them feel important. Actually, the meaning or function of banquets in Chinese business culture cannot be explained so simply.

There are many stories about both 'good' and 'bad' banquets. Two notable and opposite perspectives include a foreign China-based managing director who was quoted as saying: "they [Chinese businesspeople] eat and drink with you, then lie and cheat with a smile on their faces". This businessman has been struggling for even modest success in China for over five years. In contrast, another manager of a company from the same country, in the same field of commerce, recently enjoyed one of the most lavish banquets of his long and successful career in Chinese business. This social event coincided with the signing of his company's twenty-seventh new business contract with a Chinese firm. An outstanding result!

Culturally, Chinese people place a high premium on hospitality. A popular way to show hospitality is to lavish guests with a vast selection of exotic food and drink. Chinese food culture is famous around the world. Enjoying food together plays an important role in making friends, reinforcing the goodwill between relatives, showing respect for seniors and celebrating festivals in the course of daily life.

One must not assume that Chinese businesspeople only treat foreigners to banquets in order to soften them up. Chinese businesspeople treat every person who is relevant to their business as special, irrespective of whether that person is an official, business counterpart, potential partner, top manager, expert authority, department head, customer or supplier — all could be guests at the same banquet table. Consequently the restaurant business has become one of the fastest growing businesses in China since the Open Door reforms.

Banquets during Negotiations

Establishing a Relationship

Banquets have four main functions in Chinese business culture. The first is in establishing an initial business relationship. For Chinese businesspeople, the easiest way for strangers to get to know each other is to talk in a relaxed atmosphere. An ideal way to get together for discussions is to hold a dinner party. In a banquet, both the host and guests can easily engage each other in topics of conversation as diverse as personal life, national culture and of course, business. This is at odds with the situation in the West, where it is not recommended to talk too much about business at the dinner table. Business is for meetings or for the boardroom. In contrast, business will usually be the main topic of conversation at a formal banquet in China.

In a 'welcome banquet', Chinese businesspeople like to show their respect and hospitality to potential partners. They want to establish this relationship on good faith at the very beginning of negotiations. At the same time, they wish to get a feel for the possibility or degree to which potential partners are willing to cooperate. This is also an opportunity to assess their counterpart's personality or become familiar with their communication style. Chinese businesspeople strongly believe that this base-line information will assist the course of future discussions. The welcome dinner, of course, could become a farewell dinner if the Chinese business host finds that there is no possibility of working together because of a lack of common interest or because of the unpleasant personality of a counterpart.

Demonstrating a Capacity to Conduct Business

Most successful negotiations in China are based on mutual trust, respect and confidence. Chinese businesspeople believe that the size, turnover, performance and assets of a particular enterprise or company are important elements of a successful business equation. They also believe that the banquet table is a reflection of this standing, but more importantly, their financial power and political support. In order to instil confidence in potential partners a Chinese businessperson will first choose a suitably prestigious restaurant at which to dine. They will then invite Chinese officials or other relevant and important figures to join them. This will assist in building up a picture of their firm's credibility and connections.

While at times the banquet table phenomenon has attracted the criticism of Western businesspeople, who see the whole exercise as a costly waste of resources, the banquet table is not about excess, but rather it turns on the notion 'face protection' in Chinese society. As introduced previously, this relates to the value of 'wanting face' — a desire to establish a sense of one's financial capacity through the medium of a splendid banquet; and 'having face' — having the network to be able to invite important figures as dinner guests. Both the opulence of the table and the calibre of guests seek for, and illustrate, 'face' in Chinese business culture.

Exploring the Possibilities

Most Chinese businesspeople prefer to discuss deals in an informal setting, rather than at a formal meeting. In a sense they feel that the potential embarrassment of a public rejection represents an intolerable 'loss of face'. Consequently, they take steps to make the whole process less formal and therefore less risky. For them, it is much safer to raise possibilities or broach demands through an informal or private occasion. Under these circumstances a Chinese counterpart may not feel a 'loss of face', even if their demands are rejected. The dinner table is in fact the ideal informal occasion to raise issues at hand, or, in a creative and relaxed brainstorming atmosphere, explore new opportunities.

Taking a Break

Conflict and argument in the negotiation process often leads to an impasse. In such circumstances neither side is likely to compromise. Once this situation occurs the Chinese side may attempt to break the deadlock by holding a banquet. They believe that this relaxes the tension of negotiations and gives both sides an opportunity to evaluate their commitment to a deal. An invitation to dine during deadlock is a good sign for foreign negotiators. It indicates that negotiations are still viable. It also presents an opportunity to explore ways of circumventing the impasse.

The Time, Place and Means of Banqueting

Times and Invited Guests

Chinese businesspeople can treat their counterparts to a banquet at any time during the period of negotiations. How many banquets are held within the negotiating period depends on both the social status of the negotiating side and the success of discussions. If the rank of counterpart negotiators is high, or they are perceived to be powerful, then the co-ordinator of the Chinese group will arrange as many banquets as believed to be necessary in order to explore the possibility of cooperation. The same is true if negotiations are not proceeding smoothly. The frequency of banquets is usually only an indication of the requirement for further intelligence gathering. Generally, however, there are at least two formal banquets, the welcome banquet and the farewell banquet.

As part of Chinese banquet culture, guests are never required to pay. In fact it is an offence to offer. The same rule should also apply when a foreign counterpart hosts a banquet to return his Chinese counterpart's hospitality. Chinese people cannot understand the practice of 'going Dutch' or asking guests to contribute to the cost of a meal in their honour. This practice must be avoided. It is considered to be very stingy.

Sometimes invited guests are not directly relevant to the business at hand. These invitees may be important players in terms of the potential opportunities they represent. Sometimes these invitees are senior government officials. The Chinese like to use these special guests to indicate to their negotiating counterparts that they have high credibility and strong support. Simultaneously, the invitation of special guests is an opportunity for them to strengthen their relationship with these important figures through their exposure to 'important' foreigners.

Banquet Protocol

Chinese people prefer to allocate seating in terms of age or rank. In this respect, the order of seating is best left to one's Chinese partners. It is thought to be impolite to select one's own seating without consulting the banquet host or hostess. At official banquets the chief guest is often seated at the left of the host. Chopsticks are used for all courses in Chinese restaurants. A foreigner does not have to feel embarrassed if they are less that expert in the use of chopsticks, but dexterity and skill will cause heads to turn, particularly if you are able to pick up one, two or three roasted peanuts with chopsticks at one time. Obviously trying chopsticks is a lot of fun, but it is wise to have a fork and spoon available as a back up.

Normally the banquet formally starts by ritual toasting initiated by the host. He or she will arrange for every glass to be charged with an alcoholic beverage and then toast the entire group. A few courses later, it is expected that the principal guest will toast the entire group. Every toast is preceded by a chorus of the word *ganbei*, which means 'drink up', 'bottoms up', or 'cheers'.

Further to this, there are a number of other important aspects of Chinese dinner parties that Westerners should be aware of. The first is that according to Chinese banquet etiquette, it is the responsibility of the host or hostess to make sure that all guests are served the full range of dishes on the menu, continuously throughout the meal. A portion of each dish is first served to every guest and then made available for further helpings. In the West, it is the custom to consume as much of the individual portion as desired. However, according to the Chinese custom, a guest's plate is never permitted to be empty. As soon as a plate is empty it will be replenished.

The Chinese maintain that a banquet is not complete without alcohol. Wine, beer and other drinks are provided, but a particular type of strong distilled spirit is often served as a basic standard. Many Chinese whiskies range in strength from 30° to 60° proof. ·Chinese liquor is very intoxicating and can quickly lead to raucous behaviour at the banquet table. It is advised to take a sip and then claim not to be able to consume powerful spirits, at least before the call to 'bottoms up'. Otherwise, it will be assumed that the Western negotiator is capable of handling strong spirit and will be endlessly encouraged to toast the heath of everyone involved. In some regions such as Beijing, Mongolia and Northeast China, banquet hosts or guests can become completely inebriated without causing the slightest disgrace.

Case Study: Strong Drink and Relationship Building

One example of a way in which inebriation can be used to advance the cause of good business comes from the personal experience of the third author of this book — Rob Goodfellow — who has been called to give many toasts at many banquets in China. On one particular occasion a very important Chinese businessman hosted the dinner. Mr. Goodfellow was asked to toast this person many, many times. As the glasses were refilled and drained, refilled and drained, inebriation ensued. Mr. Goodfellow bravely charged his glass a third time and his response was as follows: "I would like to again toast the good health of Mr Huang. When I first toasted Mr. Huang's good health he looked very well, but after three glasses of Chinese liquor Mr. Huang looks three times better because I can now see three of him". There was a moment of silence as the interpreter translated the toast, and then explosive and raucous laughter. The night was a great success and lead to a long term and profitable relationship between Mr. Goodfellow and his Chinese partners.

Chinese businesspeople regard the banquet as a celebration — not just an opportunity to eat. Therefore, the Chinese do not appreciate a silent dinner guest, but enjoy a range of light-hearted conversation, punctuated by more focused discussions on a range of issues, including business.

Finally, it is a basic assumption on the part of the Chinese host that the foreign partner will hold at least one banquet in return for his counterpart's hospitality. If this is not arranged the business relationship will not necessarily be damaged. Chinese businesspeople will suspect their counterpart of being miserly, or worst, discourteous. A common Chinese social value assumes that courtesy demands reciprocity.

Chinese Negotiating Tactics

Chinese businesspeople describe the commercial field as like a 'field of battle' in which the application of appropriate tactics determines the success or failure of a 'campaign'. In the Chinese case many of these tactics are drawn from traditional Chinese warfare stratagems. To appreciate this is a great advantage. Every move is carefully planned in advance. Perhaps this is the reason why some foreigners comment that the Chinese treat negotiations like a 'war'. The tactics most frequently used by Chinese negotiators are as follows:

Knowing the Strengths and Weaknesses of Both Sides

A prominent Chinese tactic maintains 'know yourself and know your enemy, then one may win one hundred victories in one hundred battles'. This means that you must first estimate your own weaknesses and strengths and then judge these in the light of your enemy's shortcomings and succours. In this way you will easily plan a suitable and effective strategy against your rival.

A Chinese business negotiator will try and gather as much information about their adversary or counterpart as possible. Their preparation work is usually extensive. It involves everything from a detailed brief on their counterparts' business strengths and weaknesses, to planning the configuration of the welcome banquet. This maximises intelligence gathering during the first cautious steps towards establishing a framework for discussions. A Chinese counterpart will then keep smiling. He or she will at first listen intently without saying much about any substantive issue. The Chinese side will then quietly process this preliminary intelligence and incorporate it into their overall negotiating strategy.

Making Use of Vulnerabilities

Part of this intelligence gathering involves identifying areas of weakness in the other side's position or personality. For example, if the Western negotiating side has given their Chinese counterpart the impression that they don't wish to spend too much time, money, or energy on lengthy negotiations, then some Chinese business-people may purposely arrange delays thereby forestalling a final decision.

Ironically, Chinese negotiators sometimes use their own weaknesses to improve their position. They may try to get the other side to appreciate their particular problems first. They will then take a great deal of trouble to praise a foreign company for being friendly, resourceful and powerful. Subsequently, Chinese negotiators will argue that small concessions on the part of the

Western company represent a friendly gesture that is perfectly consistent with their Western counterpart's high standing. They will further argue that by conceding a particular point, the reputation of this foreign company will be promoted in China. However, it is important to note that the above may actually be true and not a strategy at all. It may be a genuine attempt to honestly convey the Chinese counterpart's lack of technological or financial power.

On the other hand, if this is a tactic, it will be employed where the Chinese lack technological or financial strength and wish to benefit from their counterpart's experience without cost. The Chinese appreciate that Westerners like to talk about themselves, about their achievements and what distinguishes their enterprise as different and exceptional. The Chinese will listen patiently to this as they absorb relevant knowledge, noting advantages and disadvantages. If this tactic is understood and anticipated by Western people they should have no trouble in using it to their own advantage.

Using Other Competitors as a Weapon

One strategy that Chinese businesspeople often employ in negotiations is to make use of their counterpart's competitors as a means of persuading them to make concessions. Chinese businesspeople will typically offer a number of hints that a competitor has been willing to provide a better offer. These hints will become more brazen as the need arises, particularly if the Chinese side feels that negotiations have become deadlocked.

Chinese businesspeople may also acknowledge that the technology or products of their prospective business partners are excellent, and indicate that they would prefer to deal with the present company rather than any of their competitors, yet at the same time suggest that another company is willing to provide a better offer for the same item. This puts pressure on their foreign counterparts to make a sought-after, but previously refused concession. This is why in forging a deal with Chinese business partners, Western negotiators must come to the table with a number of concessions or fallback positions. An intransigent bottom line position is ineffective.

Gaining a Respite

During negotiations, Chinese businesspeople are likely to employ the stratagem of requesting a respite to gather up more time in order to 'allow further progress'. As mentioned above, this is particularly true if negotiations have degenerated into deadlock or have become wholly unfavourable to the Chinese side. There are two ways that the Chinese apply this tactic.

The first stratagem is represented by the Chinese expression 'red face and white face' — or in the West — 'good guy and bad guy'. This means that during negotiations, one person plays a positive and supportive role, while another appears to do things to undermine the situation. The former is the 'red face', and the latter the 'white face' — someone who comes over as tough and uncompromising. Actually, these two kinds of persons work closely together.

There is a further strategy designed to gain time for the Chinese negotiating side. This usually emerges when a Chinese counterpart claims temporary inflexibility on the grounds that they do not have the authority to offer a particular concession. However, at the same time, the Chinese team will indicate that their manager or other governmental official has the right to do so and should be given the opportunity to carefully consider the matter at hand. In this instance,

Chinese negotiators are playing a role of a 'white face', while their managers are assuming the role of a 'red face'. On other occasions, the role of 'red face' and 'white face' may appear to exchange opposing views between themselves and their higher management. In the second instance, Chinese negotiators may say that they would like to concede to the other side's demand, but unfortunately their superiors do not agree with them. They then suggest that they need time to change their managers' minds. Nevertheless their purposes are in both instances the same, that is, to obtain time for respite or further intelligence gathering. Sometimes what they are saying is true and they genuinely do need to report At other times the Chinese are simply making use of this as a tactic.

Usually Chinese businesspeople take their responsibilities very seriously in respect to showing hospitality. This includes arranging a variety of tour activities for their guests or negotiating 'opponents'. Again, like the banquet, these programs provide respite when negotiations are not going well. Tours appear to be basically recreational and do indeed provide respite; however, for the Chinese side, business still continues in an informal but nevertheless effective way.

Controlling the Final Stage

One of General Sun Zi's thirty-six stratagems of particular relevance to Chinese businesspeople, is, to "be patient and induce your enemies to use up their resources. Provoke them, but do not attack until you have a clear advantage". Chinese negotiators will not engage in exuberant debate, strong negotiating tactics, or bitter exchanges at the beginning of the negotiating process. They will instead allow their rival to use up their resources such as time, energy and money. They will lure their opponents to expose their strengths and weaknesses. They will then fully ensure that they are in a superior position before assuming a more aggressive final assault.

Chinese businesspeople may contrast irregularities in their counterpart's words or conditions and, in particular, between what was said in the early stages of negotiations and what is said towards the end of the process. This is designed to provoke a response which may lead to a concession. In this case, they are employing what the Chinese refer to as 'hitting a rival's shield by using his own spear'. They may raise an old issue, which has supposedly been already settled, but not fully accepted by the Chinese team, especially after protracted and unfruitful negotiations. They may suggest that these irregularities have unduly prolonged the process and that negotiations between the two sides must end because the time is urgent for making a final decision. As a result, they can push all the advantages they have accumulated in the last stage by a 'surprise move'.

Case Study: Striking the Best Deal at the Last Minute

The Chinese company 'Tiancheng' wished to import some technology. It commenced negotiations with three foreign companies simultaneously, two from North America and one from Germany, Tiancheng negotiators prudently arranged separate meeting times with negotiators of these three exporters. In China, Tiancheng treated all foreign negotiators with warmth and hospitality. The Chinese negotiating team also travelled abroad to visit the three foreign company's headquarters. Here they collected the information they needed to compare the various offers. After compiling a list of the advantages and disadvantages: technology, services, prices and personnel, they found that a crucial difference was price. Therefore at the very final stage of negotiations,

Tiancheng both implicitly and explicitly indicated to one of the North American firms that the German company was offering a cheaper price, though there was very little to separate the three bids in terms of the quality of their technology. The same rule was applied to each company separately using the remaining two companies as foils. The respective Western negotiators each competed to improve their offer, as the deal itself was attractive, and cost of negotiations had been borne by these foreign companies up to the final stage. The Chinese company was able to secure the best deal in the end by using the forces of competition to work for them.

As the above case study illustrates, the Chinese use what is called in the West — *'good guy and bad guy'*, or *in China, 'red face and white face'* tactics to control the final stage of a negotiating contest. The success of this tactic lies in the forces of internal competition within the framework of multiparty bidders, however there is another important aspect to this, namely timing. The Chinese team allowed each of the three companies to expend the maximum amount of resources on negotiations so that, in the final stage, it would have been extremely difficult to abandon the process, having already com-mitted resources to costly in-country negotiations. Therefore competitors would be much more likely to compromise on price than abandon the deal altogether, thus benefiting the Chinese negotiating team's final position.

A final important point is that in China, as in the West, sometimes negotiators can be 'too clever by half'. If a particular tactic leads to an irreconcilable breakdown in what was otherwise a successful business partnership, then clearly the negotiating team did not have the necessary skills to navigate their way to a mutually satisfactory conclusion. Whether or not the tactics outlined in this chapter work in business, entirely depends upon how the practitioner applies them in a given situation.

There is no reason why, with patience and preparation, a Western negotiating team cannot exceed the culturally specific negotiating prowess of their Chinese counterparts. Paradoxically, this demonstration of acumen will strengthen business and friendship relationships and not undermine them. The Chinese recognise and respect a worthy 'opponent' when they see one.

Chapter 5

Joint Ventures

Practical knowledge of the general characteristics of Chinese corporate culture and managerial styles is essential for those foreign companies that want to conduct business successfully in China. In this chapter, the reasons for success and failure of Sino-foreign joint ventures in China are identified and the importance of cultural adaptation is stressed. To help foreign investors choose the right partners for their business, the distinguishing features of modern Chinese corporations, including state-, private- and collective-owned firms, are introduced. To be successful, foreign investors must decide what they require of a potential Chinese partner in respect to their corporate objectives and goals. They must also be aware that management in China is still deeply influenced by Confucian values. Chinese managers operate within an essentially semi-authoritarian work environment. Subordinates are expected to yield to their managers and fully comply with their instructions. Therefore this chapter covers detailed issues such as the importance of inter-work place relationships and harmony, managing people in a joint venture, the recruitment of suitable Chinese employees for joint ventures, the role of *guanxi* in management, and how to work co-operatively with the bureaucracy and the China Communist Party.

More and more Western companies are entering the Chinese market with the intention of establishing formal business partnerships with local counterparts. In the PRC, successful joint ventures are usually those that have combined both Chinese and Western managerial models. The companies that have failed are usually those that have insisted on following their own particular managerial style and culture to the exclusion of the other. Consequently, when cross-cultural conflict arises there is no effective management process in place to deal with misunderstanding and deadlock.

Finding a Good Partner

To be successful, foreign investors must decide what they require of a potential Chinese partner in respect to their corporate objectives and goals. Having done so, the foreign company then needs to ask the following questions:

- Is the Chinese joint-venture partner an entity enjoying full registered legal status under Chinese law?
- What type of ownership is involved — state, collective or private?
- What advantages and disadvantages does the particular type of ownership enterprise offer the prospective joint venture partner?

In the latter instance, there are advantages and disadvantages in dealing with each type of enterprise. The more you know about different types of enterprises, the more likely you are to choose a suitable partner.

Generally speaking, the large state-owned enterprises (SOEs) have an abundance of skilled workers, a certain degree of technological expertise, and the support of the government in terms of raw materials and financial resources. But many of them have the disadvantage of low effectiveness, a poor sense of market orientation and the heavy financial burden of employees' welfare provisions.

Collective-owned enterprises have organisational flexibility combined with an element of government support, good appreciation of market-orientation and a relatively high degree of production effectiveness. The disadvantages associated with collective enterprises are that they have less direct government support, while worker quality, technological expertise and overall performance may also vary significantly from one organisation to the next.

Private-owned enterprises have the advantage of relative high effectiveness. They are also generally free from bureaucratic interference. This group has the flexibility to hire and fire staff, and they possess a strong sense of a market-orientation. Nor do they have the financial burden of having to uphold a comprehensive employees' welfare program. However, at times private-owned organisations in China may have trouble obtaining the necessary operational resources for production from the government.

Enterprises located in rural areas tend to be organised on a town or village basis. They may be either collectively owned or in private hands and they possess similar advantages and disadvantages to their counterparts in the cities. Although they may run their operations at a very low labour cost, this could constitute a disadvantage in terms of expenditure on further training. There could also be problems associated with the potential for a foreign partner to be drawn into village-based local conflicts regarding land use.

State-Owned Chinese Corporations

China's state-owned enterprises (SOE) still account for about a third of the country's industrial output, and much more of its industrial employment. They enjoy huge support and protection from the central government. Currently, they are heavily burdened with social obligations to employees and former employees. It is reported that many of state-owned enterprises are extremely inefficient and have difficulty in surviving competition. However, there are some that have found a way to successfully compete in the market, through restructuring, entering into joint ventures and taking advantage of the substantial support offered by the central government.

Corporate Obligations

One of the salient features of management in China is that state-owned organisations play an extensive role in both the professional and private lives of their employees. Most enterprises in China not only provide their employees with working opportunities and salaries, but must also offer a full array of material necessities. These include medical insurance, housing, childcare, schooling and entertainment. Some large state-owned enterprises even provide their employees with on-site retail shopping.

The corporate functions of many Chinese enterprises are like that of a small society. Therefore most Chinese employees, or at least those who are employed in state-owned enterprises, have a very firm idea that a credible enterprise must care for every aspect of their lives, including work and family environment. Besides the usual development and operational concerns that all managers have to deal with, a general manager in the PRC must also spend a great deal of time and energy in looking after the personal and private welfare of his employees. A credible managing director must be skilled at leading a managerial team who are responsible for a childcare centre, the allocation of limited housing resources, and organising the catering for special occasions and festivals. They are even expected to conciliate in serious family and other interpersonal disputes.

The employees of Chinese enterprises regard their organisation as a 'large family'. The senior general manager assumes the role of 'parent'. Accordingly, managers receive from their employees the kind of respect normally afforded to the head of a family. In return, mangers must take care of those in their employ. If employees feel that their general manager has successfully assumed the role of a good parent, the enterprise will be cohesive and efficient. It will also enjoy high employee morale. Conversely, managers who do not live up to this basic cultural expectation will be considered a failure by their employees, regardless of how profitable their company may be. The mark of a good manager in China is not measured against management acumen and personal capacity alone but also against whether he or she can secure basic material and welfare benefits for employees at the same time as running a high-performance commercial enterprise.

The payment system of Chinese state-owned enterprises is also totally different from that of Western companies. Employees are generally paid to be in the workplace, not for performance. Second, salary is issued on a monthly basis and is normally composed of four parts — a basic salary, a seniority salary, bonus payments and a subsidy. Contents of the subsidy component of the salary package vary between regions and organisations. Generally, however, this includes a subsidy for housing rental, medical care, non-staple foodstuffs, newspapers and books, transportation, even clothing and footwear. Beyond these items other goods and services are adjusted by each enterprise according to specific policies and performances. Every employee in a Chinese SOE normally receives a monthly salary sheet that lists all salary subsidy deductions. Sometimes these items are so numerous that ordinary employees do not bother to calculate their total value. When you ask an employee of a state-owned organisation how much he or she earns every month, the actual figure may be much lower than his or her stated income. Only two salary items, the basic and seniority salary, can be easily calculated. The various other components of a Chinese employees' wage reflect the 'large family' principle which characterises most Chinese state-owned enterprises.

The fact that salaries in state-owned enterprises are not performance-linked diminishes the potential productivity and profitability of these organisations. In order to circumvent this institutionalised handicap, many SOEs, since the early 1990s, have restructured their operations and formed subsidiaries where salaries are directly linked to performance and competitiveness in the market place. These subsidiary enterprises are required to submit a certain amount of their revenue to the parent organisation, but are allowed to keep the remainder of their profits as income. Under this compromise system, some SOEs are now performing very well. Many foreign companies have targeted these firms as potential partners for Sino-foreign joint ventures.

Organisational Structure

The greatest difference in organisational structure between most state-owned Chinese enterprises and all Western companies is that there are parallel management systems within a Chinese enterprise. One is an administrative system and the other is an internal leadership organised around the Chinese Communist Party (CCP). Chinese managers often refer to this system as 'two carriages'. Before 1984, a CCP secretary controlled all Chinese enterprises. After the 'Enterprise Reform Policy' of that year, a general manager was also made responsible for the overall management of these firms. Since then, both the CCP secretary and the general manager have been required to exercise parallel responsibility. Disputes about who should be in a dominant leadership role in a state-owned enterprise seem to be unending. Role ambiguity between the general manager and the CCP secretary leads to confusion and even a power struggle between the two parties. This is especially true when there is a drive to disseminate political propaganda — for example, after the events of Tianamen Square, the dominant role of the CCP secretary was reinforced while the autonomy of the general manager was weakened.

The CCP is represented in almost every Chinese enterprise — state, collective enterprises and joint ventures. The main responsibilities of the CCP are identified as "supervising and guaranteeing" the strategic direction of the enterprise and participating in important decisions, especially in respect to personnel. In some small enterprises, the top senior managing director may be both the general manager and secretary of the CCP, but in almost all large, state-owned or joint-venture enterprises the position of general manager and CCP secretary are held by different persons. Inevitably, difficulties arise from differences of opinion between the two parallel managerial systems.

The "small society" and 'two carriage" structure in China's state-owned enterprises have been severely challenged by the reform process. Many state-owned enterprises afford to pay their employees' salaries. This has lead to bankruptcy, which is now covered administratively under China's new Enterprises Act.

Corporate Values
Management in China is still deeply influenced by Confucian values. Despite the Chinese government's best attempt to negate the

influence of Confucianism in the years from 1949 to 1977, its influence remains strong to this day. There are some common characteristics or management values that typify all Chinese enterprises, although, as in the West, corporate values vary according to each particular enterprise. Importantly, an interest in corporate culture has been 'fashionable' in Chinese enterprise circles since the mid-1980s (Wang and Zhang, 1989). Under the influence of Western management theorists and practitioners, a number of senior Chinese managers began to consider how they might construct their own uniquely contemporary Chinese corporate culture. These managers appreciated that this new model had to complement both traditional Chinese cultural values and the orientations of a burgeoning market economy based on commercial competitiveness. Since that time, a distinctive Chinese corporate identity has emerged, which now reflects both traditional Chinese culture and contemporary values in the context of rapid social, political and economic change.

Impersonal Achievement

Chinese managers in the state-owned enterprises insist on group or collective orientation. Requests for the recognition of individual accomplishment are usually denied. Any achievement by an individual is typically claimed on behalf of the group or organisation, although recent research indicates that Chinese employees' personal achievement motivation rating has become much stronger since the mid-1990s. As a consequence of this collective orientation, many Chinese managers adhere to a non-competitive management ethic — the only type of competition that is allowed, or actively encouraged, is a kind of 'friendly competition' between factories, workshops and individuals.

This situation is very different from many Western organisations, which are characterised by a spirit of self-actualising competition. The atmosphere within a Chinese organisation is far less encouraging for outstanding individual achievers. Chinese managers believe that they must consider the 'feelings' of superiors or colleagues who may not like someone who is thought to be trying to overtake them in the hierarchy. Accordingly, Chinese managers constantly try to strike a balance between modest individual virtues and prominence within a group. Chinese managers think that the ideal 'middle way' is for everyone – subordinates, peers and superiors, to be qualified in their position and to be compatible with others. Chinese managers constantly express the idea that individuals should work in harmony with other colleagues in an organisation and, for the sake of 'balance', should keep competitive behaviour to a level that is acceptable to the majority.

Trust

In some state-owned enterprises, Chinese managers cannot entirely trust their subordinates. Research has revealed that while Chinese managers may trust their subordinates' job maturity, they do not entirely trust the psychological maturity of their employees.(Wang and Clegg 2002) in other words, they strongly believe that their subordinates are able to carry out assigned jobs in terms of their skill and experience, but they do not believe that their subordinates are entirely willing to shoulder the responsibility for performance.

Hierarchical values are partially to blame for this state of affairs. It has been explained that Chinese managers think of their enterprises as a family system. From a cultural point of view, within this system, subordinates are treated like 'children' who are seen to be dependent and cannot ever be fully trusted to take responsibility.

The general manager is seen as a parent who must look after and control his or her subordinate 'children', even though it may readily be apparent that their employees are very capable of doing their job in terms of their skills. Consequently, many Chinese enterprises are run exclusively by a single, powerful 'father' figure, who does not think that his or her subordinates are psychologically mature enough to take responsibility for managerial work and will make most substantive decisions on his or her own. Management at the senior level may feel it necessary to develop trust in someone who is faithful and loyal, even though he or she may not be competent. They tend to pursue the development of trust in employee good faith and make this type of trust an effective way to establish vertical relationships at work.

Obedience

Chinese managers operate within an authoritarian work environment. In this 'top down' system, personal power is used to get things done. Subordinates are expected to yield to their managers and fully comply with their instructions. The conformity and obedience of subordinates is a basic cultural expectation and one that is more or less taken for granted by most Chinese managers. Nevertheless, many Chinese managers also believe in 'the relationship of co-operation in work', whereby same-status employees should assist each other in order to achieve equality in the work place. The latter principle should not, however, be seen to negate the 'obedience relationship' that must exist between a supervisor and his or her subordinates: this is an expression of hierarchy, although in China this relationship is always referred to as 'cooperation'.

The Importance of Harmony

Chinese managers place a high value on informal relationships within an organisation. As explained, the Chinese word for 'informal relationships' is '*guanxi*'. The term, however, can also be translated as 'connections'. In Chinese enterprises, 'unofficial channels', or 'connections' are used to achieve organisational aims and objectives through the dispensing and repayment of 'favours' (patronage). Compared with their counterparts in other countries, Chinese managers often pay more attention to personal relationships within the work environment than to the job at hand. Chinese managers believe that maintaining good relationships at all levels of an organisation is crucial.

Chinese managers are likely to show respect to their superiors in order to nurture 'good guanxi' in relation to those above them, while at the same time using their own position in the hierarchy in a paternalistic manner to build up good faith and friendly working relationships with subordinates.

For Chinese managers in state-owned organisations, cooperation encompasses non-work activities as well. Managers go to a lot of trouble to establish and develop private friendships with work peers, superiors and directors, beyond that required by their work commitments. If possible they like to demonstrate their concern, or offer assistance to an employee on a personal or social level as well. The 'small society' characteristics of Chinese enterprises help to explain this situation. So does the fact that employees in state-owned enterprises normally enjoy a guarantee of lifetime employment. These characteristics force managers to concentrate on the establishment of non-work relationships to the extent that this is considered a prerequisite for maintaining sound workplace cooperation.

Leadership Style

Prior to the 1990s, leadership styles in China were essentially paternalistic or authoritarian in nature. The delegation of power within most organisations was limited, with most of the decision-making power concentrated in the hands one or two top managers or CCP officials. Although Chinese administration has never been truly task oriented, and must always include an element of employee orientation, centralised decision-making is always an essential part of leadership. More recently the situation has showed signs of change. The degree of worker participation in decision-making processes has improved slightly with the introduction of a more consultative leadership style. This style has predominantly occurred in those firms that have accepted the consultant advice of outside professionals, especially those who specialise in the implementation of consultative decision-making processes. The following aspects outline the main characteristics of Chinese leadership style.

Formal Participation Systems

Theoretically, worker participation is one of the strong points of the Chinese management system. Unfortunately, in many enterprises, theory and practice are two separate things. A system of formalised worker participation has been well established in China since the early 1950s. This took the form of worker's congresses (which are actually still in place). These officially-sanctioned groups were authorised to scrutinise managerial practices; to be involved in decision-making at various levels; and to air grievances on the part of employees or offer suggestions through representatives. Workers are still directly elected to the position of delegate to the worker's congresses, but the role of delegates today is actually very modest. They are usually only permitted to participate in decisions relating to working conditions, not strategic policy.

Chinese middle managers are characterised by their deference to higher-placed authorities (Child and Lu 1996). This tendency includes leaving important decisions to senior management; an unwillingness to offer individual suggestions or opinions when requested to do so; and a reluctance to recognise responsibility for enterprise performance. Indeed, middle managers are virtually 'trained' not to make unilateral decisions — most wait patiently for the one man or woman at the very apex of the managerial hierarchy to decide on the 'correct' course of action and then faithfully carry out this person's instructions.

Chinese managers like using formal group meetings for the identification of decision objectives. Apart from the worker's congresses, there is another legislated decision-making forum in Chinese business organisations. This is the 'regular working meeting with the managing director meeting'. This usually addresses everyday problems and is normally attended by directors, heads of departments and first-line supervisors. Participation in these meetings is a formal requirement. The managing director usually dominates the meeting while the others lend their support to his or her ideas. This is typical of decision-making practice in state-owned organisations.

The Decision-making Process

Chinese managers prefer to gather the relevant information themselves, rather than rely on colleagues or subordinates — they believe that this is the most effective way to collect data. Currently, many Chinese organisations need to acquire urgent professional knowledge from outside their respective organisations, which inevitably must have an impact on this style of collecting information and the limitations that it imposes.

In order to be competitive in the market place, every Chinese enterprise must improve what it does and how it does it. With the increasing need for professional knowledge in every area of operations, Chinese managers are more aware then ever before that decision-making power must be based on knowledge, skill and capacity. This can be seen as constituting a new and positive kind of authoritarianism — the old 'negative authoritarianism', based on organisational position or political background, only required that a manager comply with a superior's immediate demands. In modern Chinese management the latter tendency is becoming obsolete. This 'new authoritarianism' is still tied to centralised control within the organisational structure, but this traditional paradigm can, with caution, be challenged through the knowledge and capacity of subordinates.

This new willingness, on the part of Chinese managers, to seek the advice of experts is intended to compensate for the manager's own lack of professional expertise and experience. Evidence of this gradual acceptance of expert knowledge can be seen in changes to wage categories within the business sector — professionals now receive much higher salaries than ordinary employees. The social and organisational benefits conferred by technological and organisational expertise are gradually being accepted by the business community, at least at middle and senior-management levels. Even so, despite the many positive changes that have taken place in recent years, senior Chinese managers continue to adopt an autocratic manner when it comes to decision-making and Chinese middle managers seldom have any substantive powers to influence the final outcome.

Responsibility for Decisions

Chinese managers believe that the responsibility for implementing decisions should not be taken individually. Many managers say that they want to share responsibility between top management and colleagues, however, in their own minds the concept of management as a whole does not include the decision-maker him or herself. This view leads to the tendency of Chinese middle managers to shirk responsibility whenever possible. Decision theory and psychology suggest that if a manager expects others to take responsibility, essentially nobody is in a responsible position, since the question of who should ultimately take final responsibility, is never clarified.

There are two paradoxes regarding who makes decisions and who takes responsibility for the decision-making process in Chinese enterprises (Wang and Clegg, 2001). The first is that collective decision-making exists in form and not in substance. This is especially true when a decision is made at organisational or departmental level. Although there are formal participation systems for ensuring that management makes decisions collectively, many top Chinese managers still prefer to make decisions individually in accordance with their relative position in the hierarchy. These managers often play a dominant role in 'consultative' meetings, which are technically integral to the decision-making process. What we see here is a centralised decision-making process, concealed by the appearance of a collective decision-making process.

The second paradox is that managers take responsibility in form, but actually make 'non-responsibility' the essence of decision implementation. Most Chinese managers are likely to avoid responsibility when an unexpected problem arises. Paradoxically, they are culturally conditioned not to make final decisions and certainly not to implement the decisions that they don't make. The charade of a collective decision-making procedure provides them with a convenient escape route — managers can use 'collectivism' as a pretext for evading their own individual managerial responsibilities, since most decisions are really made in a 'collective way' through formal consultative meetings that involve little substantial consultation.

The establishment of a modern marketing system, which is believed by most Chinese managers to be a positive reform, confronts Chinese enterprises with competition. Irrespective of whether the enterprise is a state, collective or private-owned enterprise, it must attempt to increase productivity in order to survive in a competitive environment. Individual responsibility for work, individual incentives, and challenging poor managerial decisions, are new tools that have to be gradually introduced into the mechanism of management. External forces of reform coerce Chinese managers into reconsidering their managerial values and decision-making style. These pressures have actually led to progressive management reform. This is particularly true of the following values: showing personality and capacity when making managerial decisions; taking a competitive approach to business; and sharing power with subordinates in the final decision-making process.

Privately-Owned Corporations

In the past, state-owned enterprises have been the focus of attention in cross-cultural studies (Child, 1995) because they have been the most representative type of corporate organisation in Mainland China. Private enterprises in China have received far less attention. They have only become accepted practice again in the PRC since the 1980s — when the Communist party claimed power in 1949 every business venture became state-owned. In spite of their relatively brief existence in contemporary China, privately-owned business have developed rapidly and now constitute a critical factor in economic projections for the PRC, contributing 19 per cent of China's GDP in 1998 (China Daily, 1999). Statistics indicate that the growth and effectiveness of private enterprises in the PRC is higher than state-owned enterprises. Registered private enterprises numbered around 1.2 million in 1999, with an average growth rate of 34 per cent per year since 1988. China's State Statistics Bureau documented an average growth rate in gross value of industrial output for private enterprises in China of 62.7 per cent between 1990 and 1999. This figure is 40.5 per cent higher than the national average of 22.2 per cent for all enterprises over the same period. China's Amended Constitution in March 1999 recognised that private enterprise had become an important part of China's market economy (Hong Kong Information Daily, May 1999).

Surviving and Thriving

Almost all private enterprises in China initiate their business in a highly competitive environment. One problem that they share is acquiring sufficient resources to commence business and then maintain operations. The policies regarding administration of resource allocation in China is biased in favour of state-owned or collective enterprises. Because of this, private enterprises often face severe supply shortages in terms of both finance and raw materials. The major sources of initial business capital tend to be personal savings or loans from friends and relatives, rather than direct loans from governmental banks. The percentage of capital borrowed by private business from the banks has remained low in China (Lau et al, 1999). Apart from governmental policies, banks believe lending to the private enterprises represents an unjustified risk. Private enterprises are perceived to be immature in both management and moral reliability. The owners of private enterprises are usually tough players who have to raise the resources they desperately need on their own. They have to compete with government-favoured enterprises — i.e. state-owned and collective enterprises — which have easy access to resources and already have a substantial share of the market and mature commercial networks. The tough business conditions imposed on these private enterprises mean that they must adopt significantly different organisational structures, human resource systems and business strategies.

To compete in the market, private enterprises must develop the following strategies:

- Capture a niche market: private business must look beyond the existing market place, which has long been monopolised by the state planning mechanism, and seek new opportunities where an entrepreneur can play a role in filling market demands.

- Nurture *guanxi* relationships with whoever may be in a position to positively assist their business. Such relationships may overcome the obstacles imposed by unfavourable government policies and generate quick profits. The relationships on this list will usually include local and central governmental officials, suppliers, buyers, and even state-owned counterparts. Private businesses are willing to offer huge bribes to officials and other influential persons in order to develop their business network. Chinese officials often find it difficult to refuse bribes from private enterprises, who are keen *guanxi* seekers and offer the most enticing inducements. Having said this, private businesses are not forced by individuals within the bureaucracy to offer bribes; rather they choose to do so — to them, the end justifies the means. This form of bribery is one of the main reasons for China's relatively high level of general corruption. Currently, there are only a number of Chinese private companies which have demonstrated an outstanding performance and have been able to develop a profitable relationship with an overseas counterpart.

- Seize business opportunities aggressively and quickly. This means that private enterprises must try to proactively out-manoeuvre their state-owned counterparts through their effectiveness and flexibility.

Leadership Style

It would be wrong to assume that leadership style in the private sector is more democratic (i.e. more like that of a privately owned company in the West) than in state-owed enterprises. Limited personal financial resources, combined with acute competition, turbulence and change, render the owners of private enterprises extremely cautious when it comes to expanding their businesses. Any failure not only marks them down as lacking personal ability, but may also lead them into a cycle of fatal personal debt. This makes private businesspeople feel a high level of uncertainty. For this reason they appear to draw on more traditional Chinese business styles in their governance than their counterparts in contemporary state-owned enterprises.

The results of a research project, conducted in 2001 by one of the authors of this book, supports this hypothesis. Based on a sample size of 740 managers, and covering four types of ownership, including joint ventures, the findings indicated that leadership style in privately-owned businesses was more autocratic and task-oriented than in state or collectively-owned enterprises. In their concern to reduce risks, these managers prefer to keep a tighter control over business operations. However, the research project did find that leaders in private enterprise tended to trust their subordinates more as most of their employees were personally chosen by themselves. Their managerial style is closer to that of overseas Chinese firms than SOEs in contemporary Mainland China.

Private enterprises in China today are characterised by the incorporation of management and ownership. The owners of these private companies maintain tight control over their business through direct supervision and involvement in management. Often owners are concurrently the managing director or chairperson of the board. Every important decision regarding firm business is therefore made, or monitored, by the owner (Lau et al, 1999). Secondly, the decision-making process is centralised for speedy decision taking: information is reported from lower managerial levels quickly and owners usually make all decisions on substantial matters. Thirdly, in contrast to management in the state-owned enterprises, top managers in private enterprises do not pay much attention to employees' welfare. Rather, they are extremely business-driven and are much more preoccupied with issues of efficiency and effectiveness.

Human Resources Management
- Privately owned companies (POEs) in China are orientated towards nepotism and favouritism in the management hierarchy in order to avoid uncertainty. They are similar in this way to overseas, family run Chinese business in that they advantageously position their friends and relatives, who may bring useful *guanxi* relationships and other benefits to the firm, at key levels (Lau et al, 1999). Managers believe that friends and relatives are trustworthy in good faith and predictability, even though their com-

petence is sometimes questionable, and that, in an extremely uncertain and tough environment, one can reduce business risk by hiring such people as managers (Lau et al., 1999). POE managers use competency criteria when selecting unfamiliar new employees who are not from their network but are qualified for the professional jobs. However, these employees are not likely to be given managerial positions at the beginning of their work. They are not trusted by management, however even they may be dependable in terms of competency. Managerial practice in dealing with these different groups in POEs is to avoid uncertainty and seek trustworthy employees.

It is thought that not to hire in this way would seriously hurt the 'face' of close friends and relatives and quite likely damage the company owner's personal life and relationships.

- Employment in these enterprises is characterised by high remuneration for performance, but low, or no, fringe benefits and little job security. To attract competent employees, this type of enterprise will offer much higher salaries than SOEs, but is unlikely to include benefits such as housing, medical insurance or other forms of social insurance. They would rather pay employees well for good performance, which in turn pushes employees to work harder. Many employees appreciate this opportunity to see the their hard work and high quality output recognised through remuneration. This is not the case in the public sector. Employees in the private sector do not have the job security of their fellow workers in state-owned enterprises. They may be obliged to sign only short-term contracts and their continued employment in the company depends on both the profitability of the company and their individual performance. While this encourages high levels of efficiency, it also means that employees in private enterprises are sometimes exploited.

Collective-Owned Enterprises.

Unlike state-owned enterprises, collective-owned enterprises (COEs) are established and owned by local governments rather than by the central government. Consequently, they are not fully supported and subsidised by the central government in the allocation of government budgets, raw materials, and banking support. Compared with the central government, local governments usually have limited resources and in this respect are seldom able to assist collective-owned enterprises in any substantial way. However, what they can do is to help to reduce unfavourable environmental conditions by securing reliable access to production resources and the local labour market. They can also advocate in bridging negotiations with banks for credit and in securing business approvals from other key government departments. Sometimes local governments' are able to provide newly established COEs with limited start-up capital. The most important point is that local government actively helps these collective-owned enterprises to compete in the market place and in return these COEs substantially contribute to local government revenues. However, COEs find that they have to pay a high price for the protection and support of the local government, the de facto owner of collective enterprises. These enterprises have to accept interference from local governments in critical issues of internal management such as employment, control mechanisms, and financial distribution, interference that quite often conflicts with the efficiency requirements of these enterprises. Many COEs, for example, have to take responsibility for redundant employment and an increasingly heavy social burden, problems which local governments face (Sun, 2000).

The growth and survival of COEs is based on their performance in the market place. Employees in collective-owned enterprises have fewer entitlements than employees in state-owned enterprises. As in the case of private companies, most of these enterprises do not provide their employees with housing, medical insurance, etc. Nor are these benefits provided by local governments. Instead, employees' fringe benefits are almost entirely performance linked. COEs are market driven, which means that they must be efficiently organised and employ effective strategies, including networking, in order to survive and succeed. In short, COEs are run in much the same way as businesses in the private sector. The only difference between private and collective-owned enterprises is that COEs can take advantage of local government protection and assistance, though in return they must contribute a share of their profits to the local government authority. COEs can freely, and quite legally, take advantage of both private and state-owned enterprises, because they enjoy a certain degree of governmental protection and flexibility in market transactions.

Some state-owned enterprises use subsidiary collective-owned enterprises to either make money or hold money, thus avoiding having to contribute to state revenues. They first establish subsidiaries with collective ownership. Then they authorise a particular business — usually one monopolised by SOEs — to either generate profits or else transfer funds from state-owned accounts into the COE's accounts. These COEs are allowed the flexibility do what ever they want in the way of generating profits. These extra financial resources are then used to contribute to benefits, such as employees' extra bonuses, banquets, and other business costs of the SOE. This method is seen as a clever means of creating income for SOEs, which are otherwise constrained by strict tax regulations, limited revenues, and the public services that they are required to provide, and is considered legal, at least for the time being.

Some sections of the Chinese military have been using the same methods to create revenue for themselves for years. Certain parties took advantage of military privileges and advanced technology to monopolise the market place for certain products and even indulge in smuggling operations. In 2000, the state government and the Military Commission of the Central Committee issued a mandate prohibiting any military involvement in business. However, it will take some time to implement the mandate and force inappropriate operators out of business.

Some entrepreneurs use COEs as an incubator to develop their own private business interests. Historically, up until the mid-1980s, to be involved in commerce, as a private individual, was still regarded as something of a social disgrace and people had difficulty in even registering a business for private ownership, let alone accessing the necessary materials and resources to start one up. Government interference was another inevitable constraint. In response, some entrepreneurs registered their business as collective ownerships in order to secure local government support and protection, as well as to gain easier access to business facilities and resources, including banking and premises. However, the problem remains that these COEs like private businesses, are not eligible to receive initial capital from local government (though they are not expected to contribute to local government revenues either). To be registered for collective ownership, these essentially private enterprises must often bribe local officials to lie on their behalf. This remains one of the reasons why bribery and corruption continues to flourish in China.

In well-established fields, such as the manufacturing industries, a state-owned or collective-owned enterprises might be a good choice as a partner. For businesses involving new technology or those with an eye on the finished-products market place, a POE might be a better choice. However, it must be stressed that with changes in government policies, COEs are declining. If the selected potential partner is a government owned enterprise, the foreign firm needs to find out what governmental ranking this enterprise enjoys. The firm may be connected to the state, to the province, to a municipality or local city government. The foreign partner also needs to find out the professional capacity of their Chinese counterparts. How much power does your partner have to access supplies and raw materials? Do they have the capacity to assimilate a foreign technology package?

A critical factor when considering collective enterprises is just how well the particular collective enterprise deals with local government and suppliers. Relationships are not always cordial between local government and the business community, collective or otherwise, and this needs to be thoroughly examined before making any decision about possible joint venture partners.

Finally, foreign joint venture partners must thoroughly investigate the financial capacity of their Chinese counterparts. Many state-owned enterprises can be burdened with heavy financial liabilities, as indicated above. Venturing with private enterprises could also be risky, especially if they have difficulty in obtaining financial support or exercising control within their organisational structure.

International Joint Ventures

Currently, there are four types of foreign businesses in China:

- Wholly foreign owned enterprises
- Equity joint ventures
- Cooperative joint ventures with legal status; and
- Cooperative joint ventures without legal status.

Chinese government statistics indicate that the establishment and development of these four types of business venture in China have been dramatic. In 1982 there were 282 foreign manufacturing companies operating in China employing some 78,000 people. By 1995 the number had reached 59,311 firms, an increase of 200 times in thirteen years. Similarly, the gross industrial product of joint ventures, which in 1985 stood at US$2.71 billion, increased to US$1,202.11 billion by 1995, a growth of 500 per cent. Furthermore, as mentioned in Chapter One, from 1980 to 1997 the Chinese government approved 300,000 discrete foreign investment projects with a staggering total actual foreign investment of over US$212.2 billion.

The rapid increase in joint venture partnerships in China would appear to indicate that China both welcomes and needs foreign investment. This may lead many foreign investors to assume that it is relatively simple to succeed in the Chinese market place. Such an assumption is misplaced — the reality of doing business in China is not simple. Many foreign business-people are successful, but only after they have experienced considerable frustration, either in dealing with their Chinese counterparts or with a succession of unanticipated and un-quantifiable risk factors.

Whether a joint venture in China is successful or not depends almost entirely on the foreign investor's capacity to adapt to Chinese business culture. The process of establishing and promoting a joint venture in China is a one of culture shock and ultimately involves the mixing of two styles of management — Western and Chinese.

These economic and cultural risk factors can cause many difficulties for foreign businesspeople, especially if these factors are not clearly signposted and anticipated along the way. In other words, to be a successful foreign investor in China, you first need to understand the differences between yourself and your Chinese partners, and then prepare effectively to overcome any difficulties that may arise from these cultural differences.

Initiating a Joint Venture

Obtaining governmental approval and support is a crucial factor in ensuring the success of a joint venture in China. A joint venture cannot be set up without government approval and cannot effectively run as a profitable business without official support. The State Council and appropriate provincial and local authorities are responsible for processing applications for permission to register a joint venture if the Chinese partner is a large, state-owned enterprise or is controlled by a provincial authority. At present, the Chinese government requires that any joint venture project with a capital investment of over US$10 million in the relatively well-developed eastern region of China must first be approved by the State Council. In order to encourage foreigners to invest in the mid-west of China, the State Council drew up a new policy in July 1996 which stipulated that joint ventures under US$30 million capital investment in China's underdeveloped regions need only be approved at provincial government level. In addition the amount of foreign capital investment for any joint venture must not be less than 25 per cent of overall capitalisation with a further stipulation that 70 per cent of the joint ventures' products must be exported abroad.

Business Approval

Normally, there are four steps to achieving approval for the establishment of a joint venture in China. The first step is to present a proposal to the appropriate government agency. This proposal must include the type and amount of investment involved, the major products and the scale of operations of the joint venture, and the proposed duration of the enterprise. The foreign partner is also required to provide the following information to the appropriate governmental departments: the registered name of the company, the country of origin and legal address of the foreign firm as well as its certificate of accounting credit and a detailed explanation of the proposed scale of operations.

The second step is a feasibility study. This normally includes the economic significance of the investment, market demand, an estimation of the required necessary resources and raw materials, proposed project location, proposed factory conditions, environment protection measures and a projection of what number of workers and staff the proposed project will require.

After approval of the proposal and feasibility study, the foreign and Chinese counterparts can begin to draft the joint venture agreement. This agreement is considered a legal document and must be in both Chinese and the language of the foreign partner. The agreement should state the obligations and rights of both parties. One problem usually encountered at this stage is deciding just how much each partner will contribute to setting up the joint venture. Normally the Chinese side would hope that the foreign partner's contribution would be at least substential capital in direct investment and the provision of technological know-how (the two items that the Chinese normally do not have). On the other hand, the Chinese partner will be expected to contribute most non-cash items, such as land, existing buildings, equipment and office utilities. The foreign partner must carefully consider their assessment of these needs.

Once the contract is signed, the Chinese side will petition the Administration Bureau of Industry and Commerce for an operating license. Upon the granting of this license the joint venture will be registered with the Chinese Tax Bureau and Customs office and issued with a banking certificate. This records the proposed amount of investment capital involved in the project. On completion of all these activities the enterprise will be officially recognised.

Government Support

Although a registered joint venture has the autonomy to control its own management and operations, there are many issues that directly involve the government. They include recruitment of staff, obtaining a bank loan, the purchasing of scarce raw materials, transportation, telecommunications, and even water and electricity supplies, all of which are important operational considerations requiring the direct involvement of government. Both the foreign and Chinese partners of the joint venture must make every effort to secure governmental support at these levels. How to deal successfully with officials will be the subject of Chapter Six.

Choosing the Right Chinese Employees

China's current labour policy provides the opportunity for foreign partners to freely engage the best-qualified employees for their joint venture or offices with a minimum amount of interference from the state. Before the Open Door reforms, everyone in China had their job pre-arranged by the government after reaching working age, or following their graduation from secondary school or university. This was especially true for anyone who held a degree. These people were carefully allocated a vocation consistent with the government's centralised labour market planning. One of the most important changes that followed the Open Door reforms was that both government and the business community now accept the idea that labour itself is a type of commodity with a monetary value that can be exchanged in the market place. This idea has had a strong impact on people's work-related values. Many Chinese people now realise that they can freely choose their preferred job according to the market value of their skills and experience. This view has challenged the system of state-guaranteed, lifetime employment, often referred to as the Iron Rice Bowl.

The Selection Process

Normally, there are six formal ways of selecting employees for a new joint venture in China.

- The Chinese partners may provide staff who are already familiar with the relevant field.

- By advertising personnel requirements on the Internet, using services such as FESCO and Qian-cheng web sites and the like — many qualified young people in China today use this source when searching for jobs.

- By using the services of a government-run employment agency (Personnel Exchange) and service centre. These are usually called Service for Foreign Enterprises Companies. These centres exist in almost in every city and province in China, and are mostly government-sponsored. They hold personnel files on individuals and can organise personnel exchange negotiations and provide information on job opportunities for both applicants and employers.

- Through regular conferences with the Personnel Exchange. Governmental departments or private companies also sponsor these initiatives. Organisations include The China State Education Commission and The Provincial Education Commission. These groups hold extensive seminars for both job seekers and job suppliers, particularly for final year university students, usually held in April or May. A variety of enterprises and organisations fulfil their recruitment needs through such meetings.

- Through newspaper advertisements. This means has recently become an acceptable and effective method of attracting key employees. The advertising fee varies between different newspapers; the more popular or prestigious the newspaper, the higher the fee. For example, a newspaper like The Beijing Youth is the preferred publication for recruitment advertisements because of its popularity with Beijing's young residents. Consequently, the price of advertising in this newspaper is very high.

- Using the services of a head-hunting company. These firms specialise in attracting high-quality professional staff, often with specialised training. The people who work for these firms are usually proficient in English and have a rich knowledge of the Chinese job market, joint-venture operations and the special needs of foreign firms. Naturally, this service is more expensive than other options, but may be the most effective way to locate senior executive staff.

Key Milestones in Recruitment

Foreign businesspeople need to keep a number of things in mind when recruiting Chinese employees. The first is that although it is not difficult for a joint-venture company to recruit ordinary skilled workers in China, it is rather more difficult to recruit highly-qualified staff, such as marketing managers and other senior executives with a background in corporation law, finance, and general or human resources. While there are many skilled and experienced workers in the labour markets of middle and large-sized Chinese cities, there is an acute shortage of professionals.

Before 1986, China's educational system provided few management training opportunities — there was, for example, no MBA degree offered in China until the early 1990s. For this reason, graduates of MBA or other managerial professional courses have been heavily targeted by many of China's largest private or foreign companies. At present the MBA degree is very popular among young people, but in terms of student turnover, it falls a long way short of meeting the present demand for business graduates generated by China's rapid economic development. Currently, thousands of young Chinese people go abroad each year in pursuit of this qualification.

It is often difficult to persuade top Chinese managers who are trained in state-owned enterprises to recruit marketing, financial or general management professionals. These old school managers have not realised the importance of employing professionals in running a market-orientated organisation. They are still strongly influenced by the philosophy of a centralised, planned economy and have not acquired a well-developed sense of competition and management effectiveness. Rather, they are concerned with product quality issues, or the state-planning index for their particular product.

Local governments in every large Chinese city have their own regulations relating to the recruitment of people from other provinces. Workers from other areas can be recruited to distant joint ventures only when they have been granted a 'Location Employment License'. The Bureau of Labour in each city is responsible for issuing these licences to non-local workers. The purpose of these regulations is to protect local employment opportunities.

The recruitment of senior Chinese managers by foreign companies or representative offices must be approved by the relevant governmental organisation. In Beijing and Shanghai, for example, it is the Service for Foreign Enterprises Company (a government agency), which is responsible. The personnel recruitment details of each new employee, including employer provisions, must be officially recorded. Chinese employers in joint ventures or foreign companies must pay a service fee to register. To avoid this expense and further administrative trouble, some joint-venture employers recruit their managers through informal channels — for example, through the recommendation of a business colleague or by a member of a professional network. However, foreign companies must be careful when recruiting in this way, as it is considered to be illegal in China, and is subject to criminal prosecution.

Chinese companies normally do not display the salary related to the advertised position in recruitment advertisements. This is usually negotiable on application.

It is most important to be patient and flexible when looking for high-quality personnel. As mentioned, China's economic and political system is highly bureaucratised and complex and has been this way since ancient times. Consequently, a bureaucratic mindset has become as much a part of traditional Chinese values as

Confucianism. This may be frustrating at times, but without the support and assistance of government officials no business in China can run smoothly.

The concept of what constitutes a qualified senior manager in China may be totally different from that of many Western countries. According to the standards of most Western businesspeople, an effective marketing or general manager is someone who posses a good knowledge of the market place or has a good background in finance, sales and promotion strategies, or a particular field of technology. Unfortunately, when it comes to doing business in China, even a person who is well-qualified in all these respects may fail as a manager if they are not able to forge and facilitate a good working relationship with the Chinese bureaucracy. Finding a confident and skilled manager who has experience in dealing with bureaucrats, and who is at the same time efficient and trustworthy and possesses a high degree of professional knowledge, is crucial to the long-term success of any joint venture in China today. Regrettably, given the acute shortage of trained managers in China at present, finding this type of person often takes a great deal of time and effort.

Ongoing Management

The huge political, economic, administrative, environmental and cultural differences that separate China from other countries are still seen as unjustifiable risks by many foreign investors. In order to run a successful joint venture, one must first have a clear understanding of potential differences in strategic objectives, as perceived by foreign partners on the one hand and their Chinese counterparts on the other.

Strategies and Cultural Adaptation

Often Chinese and foreign partners are aiming for different strategic objectives when forming joint ventures, which results in the two parties making significantly different contributions to the partnership (Yan, 1999). Foreign firms, American for instance, pri-oritise earning a profit in China or penetrating the Chinese market. In contrast, the Chinese in most cases put the acquisition of advanced technology or management skills as their top priority. In Chinese tradition, and also in modern Chinese thinking, it is wiser to learn about and appropriate new technologies from developed countries, rather than pursue limited, short-term, profit-driven goals, for it is believed that the acquisition of new technologies and management skills will ultimately lead to profits in the future.

Actually, there is no real conflict involved in these two types of strategic objectives, in that the interest of Chinese partners in acquiring advanced technology is ultimately designed to guarantee profit in the long run. Clearly, profitability, as a shared strategic interest, lays down a common ground for the collaboration of both parties — both Chinese and foreign. It should therefore be possible to achieve both these strategic objectives simultaneously.

Differences in long-term versus short term strategic objectives may also lead to conflict about how to use profits. Foreign partners, who usually provide the joint venture with financial resources, want a quick return for investment, while Chinese partners like to reinvest profits directly into the enterprise.

Another potential difference between foreign and Chinese partners is in defining the intended market place for goods and services — whether one should focus solely on China's own domestic market or extend one's horizons to include markets outside China as well. Earning foreign currency has always been a major objective of Chinese enterprises, although this desire has diminished somewhat with China's recent strong domestic growth. Consequently, Chinese partners are typically export-oriented, whereas foreign partners are preoccupied with the massive local market and are import-oriented. Many Chinese enterprises try hard to reduce imports and as a result conflicts may occur between the two parties over the use of profits (Glasser and Pastore, 1998).

Chinese partners prefer to be the majority shareholders in any joint venture. Foreign partners are dissatisfied with less than 50 per cent of the shares because they feel this undermines their control. Case studies indicate that successful Sino-foreign joint ventures must often take several steps before they reach a satisfactory modus operandi (Martinsons and Tseng, 1999). Many joint ventures start out with the Chinese partners as the majority shareholders, or else with equity shares divided equally between the Chinese partners and their foreign counterparts. This situation persists during the period of inter-partner learning, but with the growth of the business, obtaining a controlling number of shares becomes a major concern of both parties. Finally, either side will naturally seize any opportunity to gain complete control over the whole enterprise.

Comparitive J-V Strategic Objectives

U. S Partners' Strategic Objectives	Chinese Partners' Strategic Objectives
Make a profit in China	Acquire advanced technology
Penetrate the Chinese market	Make a profit
Pursue business growth	Acquire management expertise
Develop a base for low-cost sources	Earn foreign exchange through exports
Establish a presence in China	Substitute imports with local manufactures

Source: Yan, 1999

The reason a foreign company comes to China and enters into a joint venture with a local firm is to capitalize on synergies between the partners. Foreign firms are usually expected and able to provide the joint venture with technological know-how, operational skills and managerial expertise, as well as an entry into international markets for import and export. The Chinese partner should provide tangible and intangible resources. Including marketing channels for selling the joint venture's products and local purchasing capabilities as well as providing business premises, local technical services, and employees. Most importantly, one's Chinese partners understand the local business environment, especially *guanxi* networks, and can offer useful cultural insights, which can be crucial to running a business in China.

Reasons for the failure of Sino-foreign joint ventures can be attributed to:

- A lack attention to the alignment of partner strategies
- An underestimation of unanticipated costs due to PRC Government policies
- A poor understanding of networks, and business and foreign exchange events
- Weak cross-cultural management controls
- Weak relationships between parent companies overseas and ventures located in China
- Bad cross-cultural relationships between local and foreign members of staff
- Little or no understanding or appreciation of Chinese cultural values by foreign staff members
- Indifference to the complexity of Chinese business culture and an unwillingness to adapt

- Poor cross-cultural communication resulting in frequent misunderstandings
- No intention to trust and employ capable local Chinese employees in key positions
- No proper training for the local employees

Case Study: Caution without Cultural Sensitivity

Many international companies, including Brand X Beer, are mesmerised by the sheer size of the Chinese market. This company believed that that to be a truly international brand, it must have a presence in the enormous Chinese beer market. Brand X was one of the first foreign brewers to enter Chinese market. From the early 1990s, this company invested moderate amounts of capital in China, but without considering a business strategy based on factors unique to the underdeveloped Chinese system of commerce, including the complex system of bureaucracy. Brand X's strategy was rather to purchase established factories and take advantage of existing supply chains. The essence of this strategy was to become a market leader with limited capital risk. Brand X was in fact under capitalised in new plant and the necessary equipment to stay in a rapidly expanding and highly competitive mass-based market. Not only did they dedicate a small amount of capital to promotion, they also used their own promotions people rather than employ specialists in Chinese market psychology. Nor did they consult Chinese specialists who understood how to work with the Chinese media in order to take advantage of soft advertising opportunities. The factories Brand X purchased were not equipped with modern technology and their production facilities could not compete with that of new market entrants. The supply chains which came as part of the sale package of these outdated factories were found to be very immature, subject to *guanxi* networks, or even non-existent. Brand

X soon found market entrants from other countries who promoted their own international brand more effect-ively and injected huge amounts of capital into advertising overtook them in market share in China.

Brand X's main problem was that they did not understand the cultural and market differences between their operations in the West and in China. Because they did not make this distinction they felt, in the first instance, that it was not necessary to hire local people with specific expertise in marketing, promotion or supply chain management. In China it is said that spending an inadequate amount of money on product promotion is like throwing a handful of salt into the sea to make it saltier. In the second instance, they did not understand the importance of appointing senior people in China to manage issues that were specific to China, for example, dealing with the bureaucracy. It would have been better for Brand X to initially concentrate on the premium end of the market by promoting their own international brand, than to attempt to compete in the mass market with an undercapitalised infrastructure and a poor understanding of Chinese consumer psychology. The construction of new factories could then have been undertaken once this initial operation was profitable, the brand established, and the cultural risk factors measured and overcome.

Case Study: Cultural Adaptation

Technico is an agri-biotechnology company that has been very successful in China. Technico's TECHNITUBER® technology has captured a worldwide share of the commercial agriculture industry, primarily in the field of potato production. The company developed a rapid multiplication technology that enabled it to reduce time-to-market for new and existing varieties of potato from five to two years. This success reflects the ability to achieve facility yields of 10,000-13,000 from 500-1,000 seeds per square metre of production space, which is the current industry norm. The world potato industry is worth some US$100 billion annually with over 300 million tonnes produced each year. It is the world's fourth most important crop after wheat, maize and rice. In China, potato production is around 45 million tonnes a year and as such, China is the world's largest market for potatoes. While Technico was clearly able to see the potential of the Chinese market, the company also identified significant differences in business practices between themselves and their Chinese counterparts. These differences were considerably softened by the assistance and experience of Technico's major Chinese customer, Frito Lay (a subsidiary of PepsiCo). In 1996, Technico entered a worldwide exclusive arrangement with Frito Lay for the specified use of its technology. This assistance took the form of expert consultancy, mature relations will all levels of the Chinese bureaucracy, well-established *guanxi*, and the mutual benefits of an existing profitable operation. (In short, this energetic company was ambitious enough to suggest to Frito Lay that Technico could build and operate a TECHNITUBER® production facility in China to support Frito Lay's expansion in the Chinese market (this was after Frito Lay had built two other such facilities in the USA and Mexico). This was effectively Technico's entry strategy into China. As suggested, many of the official Chinese requirements were met with the assistance of Frito Lay and experienced Mainland China investment consultants, already associated with them, who were well versed in Mandarin and the subtleties of Chinese business culture. These specialists made the important introductions, and coached Technico executives in policy and Chinese business etiquette. They advised on quarantine issues, the importation of goods, expatriate visas, recruitment and other relevant issues. Frito Lay also provided the company with long-term contracts and financial support to assist in the development of a high quality supply chain.

Technico has achieved solid early success through creating linkages with other multinational firms and by effectively dealing on quality and service rather than just price. Technico's commitment to the Chinese market has held it in good stead with other key market players looking to collaborate with Technico in expanding their Chinese market presence. Significantly, Technico management has responded to local cultural sensitivities, just as local Chinese employees have adapted to the Technico corporate culture. This has created a strong team and as a result of these solid foundations, Technico's China TECHNITUBER® production facility has successfully entered the Chinese market and is setting new global benchmarks in crop production. Internationally strategic alliances and the assistance of local experts substantially contributed to their success.

Like Technico, other foreign companies, especially large MNCs, are also able to operate successfully in China by employing business practices and strategies that are specifically adapted to Chinese business culture. (Martinsons and Tseng, 1999; Xing, 1995). Indicative primary conditions for joint-venture success in China are:

- Building up a basic understanding of the major forces that have framed Chinese culture
- Maintaining an open and adaptable mindset for understanding different management styles

- Minimising value judgements exclusively based on ones own culture when engaging Chinese business deviations
- Knowing how to operate discretely within a *guanxi* network
- Employing capable and trustworthy local people to be substantially involved in business
- Creating a suitable human resource cache
- Soft management skills to motivate workers
- Smoothing relationships with Chinese governmental officials

Managing People

Managers in China should be prepared to mould their staff according to their particular needs. The unique characteristics of the managerial system and leadership style in Chinese business makes this an absolute necessity. It is also a basic expectation of China's new generation of professional managers, that they will benefit from exposure to Western modes of management.

Many joint ventures in China have failed because of a basic lack of awareness, on the part of foreign managers and investors, as to how a business should be run in contemporary China. Many come to China with the view that they have an opportunity to test their best management skills in a foreign context. Bearing this in mind, they often neglect to consider the needs of Chinese employees and managers as well as local ways of interaction. Ignorance of the entirely different mindsets and cultural orientations of Chinese employees and managers invariably leads to ineffective management. Many Western business partners, for example, prefer to adopt an impersonal approach, which is successfully employed in their home country, when dealing with Chinese employees. This approach, which stresses rules and regulations, performance measures, analysis systems and the notion of management effectiveness, does not encourage trust or support from Chinese employees. Western investors simply fail to understand that a pay-for-performance approach is unlikely to succeed in most Chinese work environments, where both employees and managers actively discourage overt competition, preferring to strive instead for harmonious relationships in the work place. Many foreign partners do not appreciate, for example, that the silence of a Chinese employee does not necessarily indicate his or her satisfaction with a particular way of doing things, but rather expresses their dissatisfaction with the system, in a polite way, under an unfair management.

It is found that generally there is a high rate of expatriates' early exit from their foreign assignment because of their poor performance or inability to adjust to a new environment. It is also found that there is a significantly high rate of low performance amongst expatriate managers, (Black, 1988; Kaye and Taylor, 1997). The inability of expatriate managers to adjust is costly for both the parent companies, in terms of employment expenses and poor productivity, and individuals themselves, in terms of personal disappointment and career disruption. For many Western foreigners, technically, socially and culturally China is the world's most complex place to work. Culture shock is an inevitable issue for expatriate sojourners. It is reported that some expatriate managers and their Chinese staff find it difficult to support each other in their work interaction (Worm and Frankenstein, 2000). Expatriate managers feel resentment and frustration for situations that they do not fully understand and can do little to change. It is reported that existing institutional factors are one of the main reasons for disagreement between expatriates and local managers. In turn this jeopardises expatriates' management performance (Li and Klenner, 2001).

Localization of management has been recognised as an effective solution to many of the problems international joint ventures and fully foreign owned companies in China are facing. (Li and Klenner, 2001).

Coping with the China Communist Party

As mentioned earlier, most joint ventures have an operational branch of the CCP working within the overall structure. Operations are different from solely owned Chinese enterprises. The joint venture branch is generally not a public organisation within the joint venture. CCP activities are generally not openly held in work time. Usually CCP cadres will not divulge their political status to foreign partners.

It is not necessary for foreign partners to be anxious about the activities of the CCP in their joint venture. The CCP normally plays a dominant role in most aspects of personnel management. If a foreign partner is able to establish a good relationship with their particular work-place branch of the CCP, then CCP cadres can prove to be very constructive in their efforts to ensure that operations run smoothly and the joint venture is a complete success. Clearly the good performance of a joint venture reflects favourably on the CCP as well as the non-CCP management stream.

Senior Managers

Due to the traditional Chinese respect for hierarchy, age and 'face protection', senior Chinese managers are very sensitive when it comes to the attitude of others towards them. They like to be respected and the best way that one can show one's respect for them is to consult them every time a decision is taken. It can also be achieved by asking them to attend outside meetings on behalf of the joint venture (though it must be remembered that many elder managers have a poor command of English and little technological or modern management experience).

Most of these elder managers are accustomed to an autocratic style of leadership. They like their subordinates to cooperate without question. Ultimately, they prefer subordinates to accept their suggestions without participation in the decision-making process. This is interpreted as protecting their 'face'. If the situation is not handled diplomatically, these older executives may become obstructive and seek to undermine the company's management. On the other hand, most senior managers do have a healthy regard for professionals and foreign businesspeople, and in this respect they can easily be converted into critical advocates of effective management. Once you have shown that you are aware of their position and at the same time have demonstrated your own professional expertise in front of them, they will be keen to accept progressive management and work closely with you to achieve it.

Middle Managers

Most Chinese middle managers, accustomed to a work ethos of minimal participation when originally employed in state-owned enterprises, inevitably bring this style to the private sector. The experience of many joint ventures is that Chinese middle managers do not show a positive attitude towards participation in the decision-making process; nor do they like to take responsibility for any stage of operations. They often keep silent when their personal opinions are sought; wait for the decisions of higher management; and shirk responsibility for implementation.

Chinese managers, and indeed workers for that matter, generally have a poor concept of quality management or quality control. Many foreign manufacturers complain that a great deal of their time and effort is taken up in constantly addressing issues of maintaining standards and product consistency. This problem highlights the need to implement progressive, and culturally appropriate, Total Quality Management (TQM) programmes in Chinese industry, extending from management down to the workplace.

The negative attitude of middle managers towards participation does not mean that they lack good ideas about quality improvement. Actually, most of them have a great deal of experience and knowledge in their particular field and understand subordinate issues very well. These middle managers can potentially become very capable and active supporters of a joint venture, if a suitable corporate culture can be created that encourages decision-making participation. To ensure this, the company should provide a detailed job description to clarify each manager's rights and obligations, though it is impossible to cover every aspect of employment. It is important to create a corporate culture that contains some advantages of Western management and is, at the same time, acceptable to Chinese members of staff. A harmonious and more democratic corporate culture can be best established through close contact between foreign and Chinese management teams from the very beginning including, as mentioned, a TQM program. A period of intensive workplace training in the operations room of the foreign partner's home organisation is invaluable and will do a great deal to convince Chinese middle managers about the importance of their participation in joint venture decision-making and policy implementation.

There is a special group of Chinese managers worth noting. Known as 'local elites' these individuals have grown up with developments and advancements of joint venture operations and have become very competent professional managers. Much of their experience has been received 'on-the-job'. They have obtained business knowledge and management competency that equals or surpasses many expatriates, who, to a certain extent, have to cope with issues of language and a lack of familiarity with business operations in China (Li and Kleiner, 2001). These local elites are well educated and better trained than most of their contemporaries. They have no choice but to survive and succeed in their chosen foreign company because they are outside the Chinese employment system, which otherwise provides housing, medication, and the guarantee of lifetime employment. These managers cannot return to the state system. To do so would mean admitting failure and a loss of face. These managers therefore tend to be both ambitious as well as adventurous. They are well educated in the field of marketing and their management knowledge is quickly and easily adapted between business networks and across industries, enterprises and regions. Their competency and ambition are entirely different from the stereotype that local Chinese managers are timid, and inferior in skills, business knowledge and economic status (Peill-Schoeller, 1994). This group must be treated fairly in relationships with expatriates in terms of managerial position and salaries. Failure to follow this usually results in these skilled managers either not contributing to the company according to their full potential, or else leaving the company taking key business networks and customers with them. Young, well qualified Chinese managers employed in international joint ventures are often considered to be 'frequent fliers' in that there is a very high rate of turnover motivated by competitor offers of better salary or positions (Goodall and Willem, 1998).

Managing Employees

First-line Chinese employees are an exceptional group. They are deeply influenced by the traditional values of loyalty, kindness, collectivism and hierarchy. In particular they have a strong sense of the virtue of repaying kindness or favour. They are completely loyal to higher management and have total commitment to the goals and objectives of their enterprise, particularly if they feel their managers are able to take care of their special needs. It is found that many Chinese staff in international joint ventures feel that they are actually working for specific persons, for example, their foreign managers, not for a company per se. They believe that personal relationships are more important than the company accomplishment (Worm and Frankenstein, 2000). They pay more attention to nurturing relationships with both management and peer than to the performance of their company. Foreign businesses should therefore identify both the subjective and objective needs of their Chinese workers as well as those of lower and middle management. This includes issues of workers' welfare and 'face protection'. Although one does not have to follow the welfare model of Chinese state-owned organisations in order to bring out the best in one's employees, it is necessary to design workplace packages that will foster an open, consultative, progressive, cross-cultural management culture.

These progressive management solutions can be a powerful weapon against a range of negative workplace values, which may, if left unchecked, adversely affect enterprise effectiveness. For instance, most Chinese workers have little appreciation of competition and self-actualisation — a consequence of the profound influence of inherent hierarchical and collective values. In addressing this problem, foreign managers must remember that they cannot expect too much from Chinese employees without first investing time and energy in training. Although Chinese employees may harbour some serious complaints about what they do and how it is done, they will steadfastly avoid saying 'No' to their superiors about job-related issues. However, they are likely to give low performance in indirect ways if their personal problems and job related issues are not properly addressed. Again this is an issue of giving 'face', both in respect to the individual employees and to their superiors.

In order to instil a culture of organisational efficiency there are two final key points to remember. The first is that training programmes, especially overseas, are very valuable — these could include technical and management skills. So is a clear employee job description, which should provide an answer to most problems arising from employees who do not want to take responsibility for low work effectiveness. Linking a productivity-based incentive programme to individual achievement is another effective means of dramatically turning around employees' performance. However, one must remember that some of these programmes are relatively new to China and though well established in the West, they will be seen through Chinese eyes as progressive and exciting innovations. The management of human resources is not well developed in most Chinese enterprises and for this reason international joint ventures need to pay more attention to the design of special training programmes for Chinese employees so that they may meet the needs of an expanding business.

The second point is that a dictatorial approach does not work well in China. Chinese employees expect to do what they are asked, but do not appreciate being shamed publicly by being ordered to perform, whether by foreign or Chinese joint venture managers. The notion of protecting one's 'face' means that most Chinese people are sensitive to direct criticism. This can be overcome by establishing a corporate culture that downplays the harsher aspects of hierarchical values and places a high premium on trust and common benefits.

Chapter 6

Using Networks

Unlike business in some developed countries where most attention is devoted to market forces, in China a great deal of energy and attention is given to establishing *guanxi* with other businesspeople and gaining the support of officials. This chapter examines how to build up a *guanxi* network and how to work constructively with Chinese officials. In the Chinese commercial community, a person's business will decline if they do not expand and maintain *guanxi* within networks. This involves communicating effectively with the bureaucracy and understanding the role of government in commercial activities.

Finally, corruption in China is a very serious problem. It occurs in all areas of business from seeking basic assistance for commercial activities to *guanxi* relationships. Although the central government is determined to crackdown on corruption, there has been only limited success in preventing its spread. The extent of this phenomenon is raised in conjunction with questions about what is the real reason for institutionalised corruption in China. Therefore the essential skills required to limit corruption as a risk factor are comprehensively and systematically covered from a practical perspective. This chapter clearly explains that without the support and assistance of government officials, no business in China can run smoothly or sometimes even function.

Although nowadays technological or academic qualifications are held in high regard, in China 'who you know' is still more important than 'what you know'. Businesspeople in China must learn how to co-ordinate their activities through the *guanxi* network if they wish to achieve commercial success. *Guanxi* literally means a good interpersonal relationship and is widely recognised as an essential prerequisite of doing successful business in China.

Guanxi

Guanxi in the Chinese context means a relationship involving a reciprocal obligation to request assistance. The commercial advantages of maintaining favourable relationships with business associates is not unique to China but the importance and depth of these relationships differs between Western and Chinese societies. In the West, personal relationships often develop from business relationships, whereas in China the reverse is true. Quite simply, interpersonal *guanxi* are a precondition of initiating any business deal in China. In the West, business networks focus on commercial exchanges, whereas the *guanxi* network in China revolves around social exchanges (Pearce II and Robinson, 2000). People only do business with those they know and trust to be able to reciprocate. Almost everyone in the Chinese business community tries to solicit commercial advantages by exploiting their *guanxi* relationships, even those who are already prosperous. Although it cannot be said that anyone who neglects *guanxi* will definitely end their Chinese business career in failure, they are likely to incur higher costs and increased risks.

As mentioned in Chapter Two, high uncertainty avoidance has always played an important role in Chinese society and culture, and it continues to be instrumental in contemporary Chinese commerce. There is considerable uncertainty attached to many commercial transactions in present-day China largely because the market system in China is still underdeveloped and not everyone is inclined to follow the new regulations and laws. Businesspeople see *guanxi* as playing a vital role in reducing this uncertainty. At the same time, there are huge benefits for foreign investors to be realised from good *guanxi* (Standifrie & Marshall, 2000). They include the smooth running of routine business operations, greater access to information about government policies, quicker receipt of administrative approvals, effective implementation of marketing strategies, and lower costs in business transactions (Tsang, 1998, Lou and Chen, 1997).

Significant Benefits of Guanxi

a) Using *guanxi* reduces the cost of choosing partners, as well as the technical transfers involved in communications, negotiations and settlements in key relationships. Without *guanxi*, a foreign businessperson must search and screen potential partners from an unfamiliar range of prospects. An appropriate *guanxi*, on the other hand, can quickly identify the right partner for any venture. This reduces the risk of fraud or deception. Information gained from reliable *guanxi* will, to a great extent, reduce the behavioural uncertainties of potential business partners, such as negative opportunistic behaviour (Standifrie & Marshall, 2000).

b) Utilising *guanxi* increases the flow of information regarding government policies. Again this reduces environmental uncertainty. In the period of rapid reforms that China is presently experiencing, there is not yet a mature system of commercial law. Local governments often adjust their policies or legislation at short notice. Furthermore, they often do not follow the regulations laid down by central government, deciding instead to further their own local interests. The central government itself also frequently changes policies if they feel this is necessary to achieve national goals or objectives. These changes sometimes substantially affect business gain or failure. Businesspeople need to maintain good *guanxi* to keep abreast of changes in policy, and to obtain the necessary licenses, permits and approvals for smooth business operations.

c) Using *guanxi* reduces ambiguity regarding potential customers and new markets. China is a huge market with a wide range of different types of customers. Identifying potential customers and placing products correctly requires guidelines and assistance. No matter how extensive a promotion campaign may be, little will be achieved, in terms of sales, without *guanxi* (Wong & Chan, 1999).

d) Using *guanxi* guarantees a buying or selling channel. It has been argued that in Chinese business, product quality, market demand, and pricing are secondary issues to be considered once *guanxi* are established (Yau et al, 2000). In China's transitional economy, with its ambiguous property rights and weak legal constrains on market competition, *guanxi* provide the opportunity to enhance a company's share of the market through improved competitive positioning and collaboration with competitors and government authorities (Park and Luo, 2001, Tsang, 1998). If there is *guanxi*, a seller can attract steady buyers and cash flow. On the other hand, *guanxi* also ensures favourable quality and quantity of goods and materials on the part of the seller, particularly if a buyer can set up a network with the assistance of officials and suppliers. A well-developed *guanxi* network also provides an avenue for building up sales based on the deferred or long-term payment of accounts. The seller benefits from favourable credit terms with extended payment periods resulting in sales growth, while the buyer benefits from a more favourable cash flow — a situation which is mutually beneficial to both parties. (Standifird and Marshall, 2000; Luo and Chen, 1997).

e) The existence of *guanxi* reduces dysfunctional conflicts between management and staff. It also secures the loyalty of subordinates by demonstrating the management's concern for subordinates' personal difficulties, thus building up *guanxi* relationships within the company (Pearce II and Robinson, 2000). At the same time, employees will feel that they owe a favour to their manager and they will be more willing to take on an extra share of work. These exchanges between management and workers leads to employees' perceptions of being members of an 'in-group' based on reciprocal obligations at the work place.

f) Applying to *guanxi* for assistance speeds up the settlement of legal disputes and disagreement. Although the resolution of legal disputes can drag on almost indefinitely within the Chinese legal system, the same problems can often be settled quickly with friendly discussion and consultation established through the *guanxi* network (Pearce II and Robinson, 2000).

g) Utilising *guanxi* assists in reducing bureaucratic red tape in the process of business approvals. Despite the transformation from a central planned to free-market economy, the Chinese bureaucracy, from the central government to multilevel local authorises, still controls most business operation. Guanxi with State officials accelerates administrative processes and reduces the overlapping supervision of Chinese officials. In other words, the unnecessary long journey of 'official seal travelling', which is mentioned in

Chapter Three, is shortened by the appropriate *guanxi* with officials.

A Dynamic Interpersonal Network

Any business venture in China — and this is true for local firms just as much as for foreign investors — inevitably faces shifts of understanding in the relationships between the various parties involved. All business relationships are viewed as an interactive process, requiring the exchange and the fulfilment of promises. Time, money and an integrated effort are required for identifying, initiating and nurturing business relationships. The skills necessary for building up *guanxi* is an ongoing process, which in the initial stages may not necessarily involve trust, but nevertheless immediately involves reciprocal obligations on the part of each player. Trust may then be built up in subsequent stages.

Friendly Contacts: Personal Connections

Businesspeople can easily extend their commercial activities if they enjoy close ties of friendship with well-placed powerful officials and other businesspeople. The best way of establishing such relationships is to make contact through a personal channel.

Normally, it would not be acceptable in the West for officials or businesspeople to talk shop after so-called business hours. On most occasions, Western businesspeople would prefer not to be disturbed during what they believe is the time set aside for their private lives. Consequently, Western officials or businesspeople rarely print their home telephone numbers on their name cards, reserving this privileged information for those who have a formal working relationship with them. This is not always the case in China. Many Chinese officials (except very senior officers of state) as well as businesspeople, not only print their name, position, title, telephone and fax numbers of their working place, but also put their home telephone number and residential address on the same name card. This format indicates that anyone can contact them after business hours if necessary.

Chinese people make little distinction between private and public life. They often put in many hours of overtime each week. For some businesspeople, their schedule during non-business hours is much more hectic than during normal working hours. It is generally believed in the Chinese commercial community that a person's business will decline if they have nothing to do, or no one to deal with, after working hours. This can be seen in the following illustration.

Case Study: Different Perceptions of Working Style

A Chinese businesswoman tried to introduce a foreign company to a Chinese counterpart with a view to working together on a China-based project. She accompanied the managing director of the foreign company to Beijing for further discussions after extensive long-distance negotiations. Like other Chinese businesspeople, the general manager of the Chinese company treated the foreign guest generously during his trip to China. However the foreign managing director found that the Chinese general manager talked almost continuously on his mobile phone — when he picked them up from the airport, at the hotel and during dinner in the evening. The foreign managing director asked the Chinese businesswomen why the Chinese general manager couldn't finish his work within normal working hours. He also remarked that evidently the Chinese manager could not be very efficient at his job. Although the reason for the phone calls was explained at length, the foreign director was still confused. He made it very clear that he did not appreciate the Chinese manager's behaviour. Ironically, while the Chinese general manager was undoubtedly busy, his behaviour may have been partly intended to impress on his Western counterpart how important, hardworking, diligent and above all, effective, he really was. Clearly, there was a marked difference between the two managers' perceptions of what constitutes efficiency and effectiveness.

In Chinese business culture, if something can not be discussed with an official or bureaucrat in the workplace or at a formal meeting, and an opportunity arises to talk to them in their home or during an informal occasion, then the manager must seize the moment. According to the Chinese, this is an efficient use of their valuable time. What is difficult for many Westerners to appreciate is that business discussed in the home or at an informal occasion is sometimes treated with more seriousness than business raised in an official forum. For this reason, it is preferable that foreign businesspeople spend a substantial amount of time becoming familiar with Chinese officials. Foreign businesspeople need to be prepared to put aside concepts such as work time and leisure time.

Expanding and Maintaining Guanxi

In Chinese business communities, useful *guanxi* have never been a single or linear connection existing for one deal only. Rather, they belong to an ongoing and dynamic network. *Guanxi* is in fact transferable from person to person and the development of individual connections ultimately leads to a network of relationships. The characteristics of *guanxi* networks in the PRC are not, as some overseas and Western researchers maintain, limited to family members and kinship based relationships (Yau et al, 2000; Standifrie

& Marshall, 2000). As matter of fact, in China, for both historic and cultural reasons, *guanxi* networks have never been solely kinship oriented. Instead, close friends, officials, old ties (e.g. previous classmates of secondary school and university) are situated at the core of a *guanxi* network. Family members and ties of kinship are still believed to be most trustworthy and relatives are often given important or powerful positions in business. However, not every family member will have valuable business connections, as involvement in commerce is still relatively new for most Chinese people, and in this respect they will not be able to make a substantial contribution to the *guanxi* network. Only a small proportion of the business *guanxi* in China are limited to family members. Businesspeople in China are easily able to take advantage of connections at any level of society and the political hierarchy. Conversely, most overseas Chinese businesspeople, as a minority in their respective countries, are culturally and politically isolated from the mainstream, and do not have the same opportunity as the Mainland Chinese to access or establish relationships with government officials. Consequently, overseas Chinese often have to rely on family or linguistic connections in developing Chinese business.

The *guanxi* network is about the cultivation of long-term interpersonal relationships in return for the exchange of favours. The more extensive the network, the more a person is proud to be a part of it and the easier it is for that person to play the game to further his or her business interests. In this network, everyone, to a certain degree, has a reciprocal relationship with someone else, and is bound to either pay back or to gain favours for others. Whether or not a person can get into a network depends on his or her current or potential contribution to the relationship. Anyone who wants to either initiate or to remain in a *guanxi* network must demonstrate and convince others that he or she is able to reciprocate in terms of being able to provide substantial assistance towards the furtherance of business operations, including financial contributions. Hence, people need to continuously spend time and money, and do whatever is necessary to nurture and expand the relationship network, even during times when there is no ongoing business between the parties involved. Forms of behaviour used for nurturing and expanding the *guanxi* network include sending gifts during festive seasons, having banquets to celebrate friendship, helping to develop new businesses, making introductions to new *guanxi*, and providing free holiday trips including chances to go abroad. Relationships in the network are carefully ranked and nurtured, according to the relative importance and status of the individual parties who are involved in the network.

Guanxi is highly transferable from one person to another in this kind of Chinese network. However care must be taken not to damage existing relationships, and to avoid creating competition from the same sources, when a particular relationship is about to be transferred. The first concern is whether a new introduction to one's own personal network can follow the required rules of reciprocity. It is believed that the reputation, not only of the newcomer, but also of the person responsible for making the introduction, will be damaged, if a newly introduced party to a particular *guanxi* network does not follow the rules. If the rules of reciprocity are not followed, then the possibility of future exchanges within the particular *guanxi* network for the newcomer will be blocked. He or she will be deemed untrustworthy and not qualified to stay in the *guanxi* network. As for the introducer, his or her reputation in the *guanxi* network will also suffer and other members of the network will adopt a more cautious attitude towards this individual in the future. In this case a 'loss of face' is likely to occur.

The second concern is how much *guanxi* should be kept to oneself and how much should be shared with others. *Guanxi* for businesspeople has a business value, which can be ranked. *Guanxi* are always closely linked to business strategies and advantages and each individual relationship represents a set of unique business opportunities. People in a *guanxi* network cautiously introduce new members into their network in order to enable them to take advantage of exclusive information and privileges, which are directed by particular connections towards themselves.

A question often faced by the Westerners working in China is whether they should be prepared to work towards entering the Chinese *guanxi* network system. Experience suggests that although it is very hard to do so, it is not impossible. Cultural and linguistic barriers are one of the first hurdles to overcome. It has been suggested that Westerners best not pretend to be Chinese. (Tsang, 1998). Nevertheless, they can clearly benefit from learning the Chinese language, which will enable them to understand more and gain greater insight into Chinese culture.

Gift-giving

For foreigners, the cultural logic and social practices of gift-giving present one of the most difficult lessons in learning how to 'do business right' in China. Not surprisingly, many Westerners who are unfamiliar with Chinese culture often make the easy identification of gifts with bribes and allege that the Chinese are promiscuously corrupt in their business practices. Such an easy identification is, however, incorrect. (Steidlmeier, 1999 p: 121).

Gift-giving is a prevalent social custom in China in all areas of life, not only within the family and between friends, but also when dealing with the political authorities, social institutions and businesspeople. It is widely used by most Chinese people to fulfil a variety of social obligations and functions. Likewise, it serves to build *guanxi* in the business world. This complex custom is closely linked to a number of culturally prominent values, including collectivism, the notion of 'face', reciprocal relationship and the importance of rites (*li*), all of which support and enhance the custom of gift-giving.

Firstly, gift-giving in China (on most occasions) is simply about following cultural norms of courtesy. It is rooted in cultural values of what is understood in China as righteousness and benevolence. On the surface, gift-giving is similar to the American custom of tipping and the Japanese practice of deep bowing. On a deep level, its role in Chinese society is as important as the banquet is to business culture, but it is more popular than the latter as it is easier and less expensive to arrange (although in China, gifts can also be very expensive). As a courtesy, a range of occasions require the presenting of gifts, including paying a visit to friends, parents, and relatives, or attending festivals and other celebrations.

This custom not only profoundly influences Chinese social life (sometimes to an extreme or destabilising extent), it also extends to establishing work and business relationships. In the workplace, there are many events that require the giving of gifts: a colleague's wedding, a graduation, a child's birth, the celebration associated with moving into a new house, and so on. Failure to give the right gift in the right way, at the right time, or the failure to give a gift at all, may lead to a 'loss of face' in work and business. Often ordinary workers cannot afford to meet their entire gift-giving obligations from their basic salary alone, especially if the worker has many simultaneous obligations over a short period. Consequently, a Chinese worker may have to borrow money in order to buy gifts simply to enhance or protect his or her 'face'. This custom is a particular feature of Chinese customer psychology — the impact of gift-giving on consumer behaviour will be discussed in Chapters Seven and Eight.

Secondly, gift-giving forms a natural dynamic in important relationships. In the West, gift-giving indicates that '*I* remember you and care for you'. In China, gift-giving highlights that '*you*' are respected by me; or that '*we*' (the giver and the recipient) are both qualified members of the group and that the giver is part of a group. This rite shows that a relationship is valued. Through gift-giving, good will, gratitude, respect and honour towards others is expressed. Under these circumstances, gift-giving constitutes the giver's necessary, positive and deliberate desire to create and maintain useful relationships. Steidlmeier (1999: 122) remarks, "In China, gift-giving forms part of a large picture: belonging to a network of personal relationships (*guanxi*)".

Finally, reciprocity of gift-giving is normative behaviour in the cultural context of Chinese business. Once a receiver accepts the gift, culturally and morally that means they have agreed to commit themselves to the giver's 'requirements' and furthermore to repay other favours in the future. In other words, the receiver is bound to reciprocate. The act of gift-giving also means that the both sides feel that there are possible grounds on which to build up trust between parties. Positively using gift-giving as a gesture of friendship or goodwill in order to establish and nurture relationships is morally acceptable in China. Indeed, it is believed that gift-giving is one of the best ways to achieve this purpose. Obviously gift-giving forms an integral part of establishing and maintaining the dynamic *guanxi* network. As stated, some Westerners ignore this cultural courtesy or incorrectly interpret the custom as a form of bribery. Conversely, the Chinese side in a cross-cultural exchange will often interpret the lack of gift-giving protocol as evidence of either a poor understanding of business courtesy or even stinginess.

Occasionally gifts serve as a token for monetary remuneration. On most occasions gifts are of significant monetary value as well as being symbols of respect and esteem. The social value of the gift is thought to be more than its actual monetary value. However, an inferior or low value gift must still be avoided, especially if the relationship is highly valued. Many Chinese like to say 'A thrifty gift cannot show my great esteem for you', when a quality gift is required. Determining the appropriate value of gifts should be carefully calculated in terms of the prospective recipient's status and capacity to enhance business opportunities. Many Westerners working in China are puzzled by the fact that the Chinese people have developed gift-giving into a 'science', complete with a sophisticated system of calculating value (Standifird and Marshall, 2000).

A low quality, tasteless or inappropriate gift will embarrass both the gift-giver and receiver. In China, gift-giving is related to the cultural values of 'face' and hierarchy. Accordingly, the type and value of a gift should reflect the status, rank and taste of the recipient. Equally, the value and quality of the gift should match the status and income of the giver. Higher-ranking people expect to receive more expensive presents than lower-ranking people, especially if the recipients are members of a group in the same social hierarchy. If a giver has a high income then he or she must give a gift of relative high value, otherwise he or she will be thought to be stingy or miserly. If he or she has a low income, but gives a valuable or thoughtful gift, then the receiver will think that the giver is generous and takes their friendship seriously. In this case, both the 'faces' of the giver and receiver have been protected. Another reason for valuable gifts is that the giver anticipates that he or she intends to ask a big favour from the receiver. Taking all factors into account, givers should choose the right value gift or gifts and plan to give the gift on the right occasions within the appropriate social context. Expensive liquor, wine, cigarettes, and valuable works of art or craftsmanship are most usually exchanged as gifts between ordinary Chinese people.

In Western countries, a gift receiver normally opens the gift in front of the gift-giver and others so that he or she can demonstrate his or her appreciation for the giver's generosity. In contrast, Chinese people do not open gifts in front of the giver. They believe that opening a gift in front of the giver is impolite. They think that this action indicates that they are either greedy or want to evaluate the gift publicly and therefore risk offending both the giver and the receiver. For the same reasons, a Chinese official will occasionally appear unwilling to accept a gift. Generally this is a display of either caution or courtesy, and the giver is expected to persist with the offer.

Amicable Relationships With Officials

One of the vital aspects of doing business in China is dealing with officials. Most foreign businesspeople say that they feel uncomfortable having to work so closely with government at an operational level. They often complain about having to deal with what seems to be an army of bureaucrats when attempting to establish or promote their business. This situation arises because most Westerners do not understand the role of the government in the commercial life of the PRC, nor do they appreciate that in China government systems permeate business at every level.

For most Westerners, their first reaction to official involvement in business is a state of culture shock. They are confused at being expected to show respect for officials without reservation. They object to giving gifts to government functionaries because they believe that it could be interpreted as corrupt behaviour. However, confusing or infuriating this may be, no matter how foreign businesspeople feel, this is an unavoidable feature of doing business in China. It is reinforced by the ancient Chinese business value of the importance of a seamless relationship between businesspeople and officialdom. It is important for businesspeople to work with the system and not against it. Foreign investors must communicate effectively with Chinese officials if they are to succeed in the PRC.

The close association between authority and the economy practically defines Chinese business culture. In recent years, as part of China's reform program, the government has begun to reduce bureaucratic controls over commerce where possible. China's WTO entry will further promote this process. However, it will be a long time before the impact of this is felt in real terms. To cope with official interference it is essential to first understand the economic role of the Chinese government and then identify appropriate strategies, which will enable one's business to prosper by working closely with the Chinese bureaucracy.

The Role of the Chinese Government
Since the Open Door reforms of 1978, the Chinese government has been working towards establishing a free-market economic system with a Chinese flavour. One of the strongest elements of the emerging Chinese model is that the CCP and the Chinese

government still control many aspects of the economy. Compared with developed countries in the West, the influence of the government on China's economy is powerful and pervasive. Besides functions common to most governments, China's various governmental organisations play an important role in the following five areas.

- *Joint Ventures*

The relevant Chinese governmental department is responsible for all proposed cooperation between foreign organisations, state-owned enterprises and some large collective-owned companies. This includes the establishment of joint ventures as well as foreign investment and trade exhibitions. Employees of Chinese state-owned and collectively owned enterprises must also secure permission to enter into overseas negotiations on behalf of their companies.

On the surface it would appear that a foreign company is negotiating directly with an autonomous Chinese business partner. However, in reality discussions are actually held, albeit indirectly, with the relevant government department. Behind the scenes, government officers will supervise every state-owned or large collective-owned Chinese organisation.

- *Price Controls*

Unlike Western free-market economies, China is still in a semi-free market conomy stage. For this reason the Chinese government has established at various levels, a special office called the Price Bureau. This department is responsible for generating market price policies and then monitoring their implementation. Although the prices of individual products can be determined by enterprises themselves, and are usually based on market forces, prices of core goods and services remain under the supervision of the Price Bureau. The Chinese central government argues that the market price of most goods and services must be measured and controlled in order to avoid political disillusionment with economic reforms. According to the government, 'public panic' over price must be avoided at all cost. Panic, they argue, could precipitate hyperinflation and currency collapse. Officials of the Price Bureau take their responsibilities very seriously. Amongst other activities, they annually audit the prices of commodities in the light of governmental price policies. Apart from checking the consumer prices of food, cigarettes, alcohol, and so on, the Price Bureau also regularly checks costs associated with services such as tourism and transportation. The Price Bureau has a statutory right to fine anyone whose product or service violates official price regulations. Some businesses, which provide intangible products or services, must apply for a special license from the Bureau to operate, for which a set fee is levied.

The type of products or services offered by a foreign company or joint venture also falls under the jurisdiction of the Price Bureau. In May 1998, the first Price Law in China came into effect. This stipulated that although the prices of commodities were to be adjusted according to market supply and demand, the central government reserved the right, if necessary, to control prices, especially the prices of staple goods.

- *Financial Controller*

The government mainly controls China's financial system. The banking industry and other major financial institutions are all presently owned or regulated by the state. Top executives in these industries are appointed and directly supervised by the government. Foreign investment enterprises may, however, apply for loans from the Bank of China or any other commercial Chinese or China-based bank as they would elsewhere. In addition, they can also take out business loans from any branch of a foreign bank located in China which has been issued with a banking licence by the government, or from China's banks located in Hong Kong or Macao.

The Bank of China and other commercial banks must follow official policy and ensure that any business fulfils certain basic conditions for the foreign investment enterprises. Examples are as follows:

1. That the enterprise is first registered with the Bureau of the Administration of Industry and Commerce and then obtains the appropriate operating licenses.

2. Following this, the business must open an account with the Bank of China.

3. The required capital for registration must be paid on time and legally confirmed.

4. The relevant governmental planning department must approve the asset investment of the project or enterprise.

5. The enterprise must provide evidence that it has the financial capacity to repay bank interest and capital within a specified period.

• *The Direct Management of Large Enterprises*

Currently, some key industries, such as rail, aviation and telecommunications, are not open to foreign management or investment. These basic utilities are operated and controlled by the

Chinese government. In recent years, the government has sought to decrease administrative interference in these state-owned enterprises. Nevertheless, the relationship between most state-owned enterprises and key governmental departments is still very close. The three utilities mentioned above are all examples of state-owned enterprises that are controlled by the Chinese government at central, provincial and municipal levels.

In these enterprises the government usually appoints a general manager or chairperson of the board, though they may also be 'elected' by employees. In addition, normally there is a personnel department at every level of government controlled by the CCP. CCP cadres are in charge of most enterprise personnel appointments. The CCP feels that personnel fall within their jurisdiction because the government sees the growth of business as essential to the national interest — currently approximately 50 per cent of all China's revenue comes from state-owned enterprises, which account for 70 per cent of employment in cities and towns.

• *Foreign Investment*
The Chinese government has controlled the level and type of foreign investment since the very beginning of China's Open Door policy. In May 1995, this was formalised as the State Council Foreign Investment Leadership Team. It is now the role of the Deputy Prime Minister of the State Council to supervise the many governmental departments that administer foreign investment. They include China's State Planning Commission, State Economic and Trade Commission, Special Zone Office of the State Council, Ministry of Foreign Trade and Economic Cooperation, Ministry of Personnel, Ministry of Finance, People's Bank of China, Bank of China, Ministry of Labour, State Tax Bureau, Administrative Bureau of

Commerce and Trade, Bureau of Justice, and the Bureau of Commodity Inspection.

These governmental departments are in charge of different aspects of foreign investment management. The three main areas of their responsibilities are as follows:

1. Checking and approving foreign investment projects in China (see Chapter Five) and controlling the amount of the foreign investment.
2. Supervising the legal operating activities of foreign companies. The relevant governmental departments monitor whether these enterprises and companies implement their signed contracts properly; whether they inject the prescribed amount of capital into the project on time according to the terms of their contract; whether they run their business legally; and whether they protect and maintain their employees' rights and working conditions.
3. Checking that the enterprise provides the necessary services for the establishment and operation of their business — this involves departments taking responsibility for assisting with difficulties that may occur in the everyday running of foreign investment projects.

The pervasive role of government in China's economy is reflected in a popular expression among Chinese businesspeople: 'One can keep oneself preoccupied trying to solve a matter for three years, whereas an official in charge will solve the same problem in an instant'. This indicates that businesspeople in China believe that officials of the government are essential allies whose support ensures the smooth running of business.

There are many cases where local or provincial officials have come to the rescue of Chinese or foreign companies. Officials of different departments have the power to determine which investments have priority; how and where resources are distributed; personnel recruitment and the promotion of the best-trained and most able staff. Consequently, Chinese businesspeople and managers understand that without the cooperation of appropriate officials, business approvals are practically unobtainable. They also appreciate that if they want to raise the profile of their business in the community or promote their goods or services across China, then, quite simply, they must look for ways of showing their respect to those officials who hold a position of authority or influence over their interests.

The role of the official in China is pre-eminent. It is based on practical economic and political power but also involves a number of other factors — social, cultural and administrative. These factors include the following:

1. Traditional Chinese hierarchical values, which ensure that respect for officials is automatic.
2. Business success as a consequence of a seamless relationship between commerce and officialdom — as mentioned in Chapter Two, Chinese businesspeople still believe that official power serves as a kind of guarantee for success in business.
3. The constant shortages of resources in contemporary China. The central government is unable to satisfy all the demands made upon its financial, material or administrative resources and it is very hard to guarantee that these resources (which are controlled by officials) are channelled equitably. Some officials may take advantage of their positions to further their own interests, which makes a cooperative relationship with officials even more necessary.

4. Corruption and the abuse of public office — currently the Chinese administrative system cannot effectively avoid this happening.

Finding the appropriate way to contact governmental officials is a major practical concern of anyone wanting to do business in China. Identifying and then deploying the 'skills of contact' with officialdom is a necessary first step towards creating new business opportunities in the PRC.

Avoid Political Issues

There is a popular expression, 'Focus solely on business in the commercial world'. Chinese businesspeople are likewise fond of saying that 'business is business, don't be interrupted by other matters or purposes and don't apply the rules of other fields to the business world'.

The Chinese central government, like governments everywhere, often creates linkages between commercial activities and political interests. However, officials at lower levels, especially those in charge of economic and trade affairs, and the average businessperson, are very uncomfortable about making a connection between business and politics. For instance, they normally avoid any discussion about political reform when engaging in business with foreigners, especially in the initial stage of contact. Chinese businesspeople are very concerned about following the rules of business, believing that sensitive political comments can easily be misunderstood, and that political discussions may be detrimental to their professional prospects. One of the reasons for this discomfort is that government officials are always on the alert for anyone, including foreign businesspeople, who continuously raise political issues during business discussions, even though this may be a matter of personal curiosity, and not intended to cause offence. Since the motives of such a person are automatically under suspicion, officials will be very cautious in their dealings with them. Indeed Chinese officials may decide to discontinue negotiations on the grounds that the person's motives are doubtful. Foreign businesspeople are strongly advised not to publicly, or indiscreetly, raise political topics with their Chinese counterparts. This will cause embarrassment and a 'loss of face' for both parties

Respecting Authority

Because China is a society that has a strong historical and contemporary sense of hierarchy, Chinese government officials have a deeply rooted understanding of authority and power. In China, officials and bureaucrats link a generalised respect for authority with respect for their own position in the scheme of things. At times, some officials are actually too sensitive about their own personal authority and this arouses unnecessary enmity in the hearts of people who have to deal with them, ordinary Chinese people among them. Western businesspeople must learn to conceal their dislike for these overbearing and oversensitive officials if they wish to navigate beyond officialdom. It is advisable for foreign businesspeople to show unqualified respect for Chinese officials wherever possible by arranging a variety of special activities in their honour. Foreign businesspeople are advised to make a courtesy telephone call to the official in charge of the department dealing with their project. This should be attended to on the foreign businessperson's first visit to China. After this, a dinner or banquet can be arranged so that the parties can meet and initiate face-to-face negotiations.

Another good idea is to invite the appropriate officials to visit the project office or plant on a regular basis. This creates goodwill, particularly during the waiting period for project approval or licensing. The purpose of these activities is to deliver an unambiguous message that the foreign businessperson is fully aware of an official's position, authority and power, and that they recognise and acknowledge that their support is crucial for the success of the project.

Addressing Chinese officials in the proper way shows respect for official authority. Chinese people are not accustomed to calling each other by their first names, except when an intimate friendship already exists at the same peer level. On most occasions, especially where any kind of hierarchical relationship is involved, Chinese people will call each other by their surname plus his or her position title. For example, school students in China cannot call their teacher by their first name or simply by their title (i.e. Mr. or Mrs. plus surname). Instead, they must call their teacher by their surname followed by 'teacher'. This custom is strongly upheld in all social intercourse between Chinese officials and other parties. Chinese officials definitely expect others to call them by their position title, such as Li Mayor, Zhang Secretary or Liu Director. This does not mean that a foreigner will be rejected by Chinese officialdom if they inadvertently call an official by their first name, or if they use Mr. or Mrs. etc. It does however, reflect very favourably on a foreign businessperson if he or she refers to Chinese officials in the correct way. Chinese officials will immediately feel that they are respected and this in turn will have a positive impact on future business negotiations.

Foreign businesspeople need to discover a particular official's likes and dislikes, ambitions, and special talents, if they are to successfully mix business and recreation. Appreciating this vital inside information is the most effective way of establishing a friendly relationship with officials of the Chinese government. Ultimately these relationships will make the difference between success and failure.

Treating Officials as a Network

Top-down bureaucratic systems in China impact systematically on all aspects of the commercial world. To establish a good *guanxi* network, people must treat Chinese officials as part of it. It is not uncommon that a business matter involves dealing with officials at several different levels, from the front line to the top of the administration. In addition, the current Chinese managerial system is characterised by a great deal of bureaucratic overlap. This means that to get something done, a businessperson will have to deal with a number of different departments and with a number of different bureaucrats or managers. Many Chinese companies often have several deputy directors for each senior managerial position. Deputy directors are supposed to be responsible for different aspects of operations, although from the point of view of effective management, the nature and volume of their work may not often appear to require more than one office-holder.

Each deputy director has the authority to participate in the decision-making process and to express an opinion when it comes to making a final decision. This type of organisational structure can obviously result in inefficient management. It can also cause a great deal of confusion for anyone who is trying to do business with a particular company or organisation. It is also especially vexing when there is a single dissenting voice which prevents a final decision being reached, for example when drawing up a contract. In these circumstances the project may have to be reconsidered. This situation is mirrored in governmental departments, because they have the same overlapping organisational structures.

The same type of problem can also arise between organisations. Sometimes an important project or proposal needs to be approved by a number of governmental departments simultaneously. For example, a state-owned enterprise may be a subsidiary of the Ministry of Telecommunications and also under the supervision of the provincial government. In this case, both governments have the right to manage the enterprise and to have the final say on management decisions. This situation is further complicated by inter-departmental conflicts and factional differences.

Directly contacting and building up relationships with all relevant officials or managers is the best way to operate smoothly in China. This is especially important when dealing with large enterprises or companies. Problems may occur at every level of government or management, and the only way that a businessperson can properly co-ordinate these complex relationships is by treating officialdom as a network. That is, everyone who impacts on the project must be identified and those most responsible for making the final decision singled out for 'special face', in terms of the respect and attention that should be shown to them. These officials must then be contacted in the proper way.

One can never presume that talking to one relevant official in charge of a particular issue or concern will readily lead to a settlement. An official may initially promise to support your business, but then later tell you that he or she can no longer help with your case. One of the reasons for this refusal might be because the official's colleagues, especially his or her manager, were not consulted by you in the correct hierarchical manner, or alternately were not convinced that the appropriate manner had been used in addressing the particular issue in question. As usual, the best way to overcome this problem is to invest time and effort into accurately identifying the top official and all relevant officials involved, by building up a personal relationship with the key decision makers, and by arguing your case in a spirit of friendship, respect and co-operation. An example of why one should treat all the Chinese officials relevant to a particular project as comprising a network is as follows.

Case Study: Missing One, Losing All

A foreign company intended to invest in a project. This involved buying a piece of land in a provincial region of China. On the surface there appeared to be no problems with local government approval associated with the project, especially as the administrative head of the region was approached strategically. Unfortunately, the foreign company incorrectly presumed that the head of the district was the only senior person they needed to communicate with. The project was no sooner started than it ran into serious trouble when the local general secretary of the CCP Committee raised an objection. The secretary felt that the company had ignored him, as he had not been introduced to the delegation, nor had he been briefed about their operational goals. What the foreign delegation quickly learned was that under China's current bureaucratic system, the authority of a local CCP secretary is higher than the administrative head of the local region. This particular company would not have had met any resistance from the CCP secretary if their representatives had properly contacted *both* the secretary of the CCP committee and the administrative head. The project was stopped in the middle of the development process. As a result the company lost both its management momentum and all previous gains in terms of the support from key officials.

Gift Giving, Relationships, and Chinese Officials

Every section of Chinese social, political and economic life is obsessed by the traditional custom of gift-giving. Sending gifts to officials is likewise a Chinese phenomenon. A common Chinese expression maintains that, 'an official never blames a gift-giver'. Commercial activities are regarded as a forum for establishing friendship relationships between people and gift-giving plays a pre-eminent role in this process. Officials, like everyone else, like to receive gifts, including appropriate gifts from businesspeople. In Chinese business culture, sending gifts to officials has a number of specific functions.

Generally there are two ways of sending gifts to officials. One is to send the gift to the official individually. Another is to send the gift to the appropriate department marked especially for the attention of a particular official or officials. The former is often executed in a private way in order to obtain individual support. The latter is a public display of respect that gives 'face' and therefore strengthens corporation between two organisations. For instance, during festival time a subsidiary organisation will send their products or other goods as gifts to the department that supervises it.

Foreign businesspeople are strongly encouraged to familiarise themselves with this custom. This can make the difference between success and failure in the Chinese market. If this strategy is not appropriately applied, a Chinese business partner will conclude that his or her foreign counterpart is not a person who can easily be dealt with.

Based on each specific situation, it is important to answer three questions before one decides to send a gift: First, should a gift be sent to a particular official? Second, what gift should be sent? Finally how should the gift be sent? However, it must be pointed out that not every Chinese official wants to receive a gift in the course of normal business. Many senior officials may refuse a gift as a matter of integrity. Sending a gift to this type of official may be detrimental to the giver's business and can result in an embarrassing 'loss of face'. Conversely, there are times when a Chinese official may appear unwilling to accept a gift, but is simply displaying either caution or courtesy. In this instance, the giver is expected to persist with the offer. Some gifts must be presented in public and some in secret. A businessperson would not receive any support from an official who appreciates gift-giving if the gift was sent in an inappropriate manner. Advice should be sought from a trusted Chinese counterpart. Again, high-quality, unique and thoughtful goods of foreign manufacture, or works of art, make the most impressive gifts.

ANTI-CORRUPTION SKILLS

At present, corruption in China is a very serious problem, which undermines the Chinese economy and threatens the very survival of the regime. It occurs in all areas of business from seeking basic assistance for commercial activities to *guanxi* relationships. In these circumstances, the co-ordination of business activities is made unnecessarily difficult — at times even impossible. Although the central government is determined to crack down on corruption, it seems to have had only limited success in preventing its spread. Corrupt behaviour occurs at almost every level of the economy and the administration, from the local level to national customs and security services, and senior officials in the central government.

Underlying factors associated with corruption include the government's centralised control of commercial activities; the underdeveloped Chinese legal system; widespread acceptance of the notion that there should be a seamless relationship between business and officialdom; private companies without official support from government, seeking favourable concessions from the bureaucracy; and officials with too much power or privilege. These elements combine to make corruption in China a multi-layered social problem.

Ordinary Chinese hate the corrupt behaviour of some governmental officials. Most Chinese people support the central government in their attempts to stamp out corruption. However, there is a considerable gap between the aims of the government and the reality, and at present there are many officials who continue to solicit bribes or act as stooges for the bribing of more highly-placed officials. There were over 20,000 graft cases investigated in China in year 2000 alone. The largest corruption trial involved 200 local and national officials in a multibillion-dollar scam to evade tariffs on imported cars, oil, and luxury goods.

As indicated, there are many reasons why private enterprises may need the assistance of government officials, and often a corrupt deal is initiated by the briber, who tries to take advantage of an officials' influence in the local administration to further their business interests. Bribery may be also used to seek protection for illegal business practices. In such instances, the briber may resort to a variety of claims, promises, even veiled threats, in order to 'persuade' an official to turn a blind eye to irregular business practices and generally ensure that they are not subject to investigation.

Some Chinese officials will themselves ask for a bribe, either directly or in some discreet way — it is relatively easy to take advantage of the gift-giving custom to solicit bribes. Usually, local officials who have the power to deal directly with foreign or local businesses have more opportunity to commit corrupt acts. For example, an electricity connection for an office or manufacturing plant may be delayed for an unreasonable period of time. One possible reason for this may be that the official in charge of granting a connection is indirectly asking for a bribe. The delay may indicate that his or her 'requirement' has not been satisfied.

An employee who takes advantage of his or her authority within the governmental system by taking a bribe commits a crime. *Both the briber and the receiver* can be prosecuted for this. The most difficult question to answer is how does a businessperson differentiate between a gift and a bribe. Unfortunately, or rather fortunately (for some people), Chinese law does not distinguish gifts from bribes in terms of value or quality. Rather the perceived difference between the two is very subtle and involves both cultural and economic issues. For example, the distinction may depend on the receiver's means of obtaining an item and the way in which the gift is conveyed. However, foreign businesspeople are strongly advised not to dispense with gift-giving because of this ambiguity. Moreover, it is impossible for a company to keep the moral standard on its own. There are many competitors ready to play the game and take business away. On the other hand, no one wants to put themselves into hot water by being identified as a corrupt person. To protect oneself from charges of corruption, it is essential to learn the skills of denying or avoiding bribery. This is a difficult process. A businessperson must be able to handle the situation strategically in order to gain official support without having to resort to corrupt practices themselves.

First, show respect for officials in charge by sending them an appropriate gift or gifts or by inviting them to join the negotiating team at the banquet table. At the same time you could make it known that you have a personal relationship with the most senior Chinese officials (if indeed you have). Because of the hierarchical nature of Chinese society this will send an unambiguous message to lower level officials to avoid asking for bribes. You can also indicate, indirectly, to the official who is asking for a bribe that you are well aware of China's anti-corruption laws and regulations and clearly understand what is wrong and what is right in Chinese business transactions. Of course this requires that foreign businesspeople make themselves familiar with the relevant Chinese Acts and policies beforehand.

A better way of preventing the intentions of corruption is to organise Chinese staff to deal with these complex issues on your behalf. They would know who should be accessed and how to strike a deal with the minimum of trouble. Many multinationals in China have been practising this approach for a long time. Sometimes a foreign counterpart can hire a Chinese associate who is a lawyer or law enforcement officer with a reputation for honesty and arrange for them to be introduced to Chinese officials during negotiations. You might also indicate, directly, that you are actively pursing various partners in China and would readily turn to other companies and governmental departments to conclude a deal, rather than be obliged to become involved in a potentially embarrassing corruption situation.

A sound way of dealing with corruption is to offer legitimate alternatives based on business success (Steidlmeier, 1999). You can explain that your side cannot meet the 'personal requirements' of the corrupt official, but suggest that legitimate work-related benefits can be offered instead, in the form of productivity bonuses. A domestic training program, or overseas short-term business inspections, can also be options.

A third way to deal with corruption is to tell the official concerned about your own personal limitations in this matter, both in terms of your seniority within the company that you work for and your own country's laws in respect of meeting his or her 'personal requirement'. You should then suggest that both parties report this 'new information' back to the headquarters of the company before a final decision can be made. It is a good practice to make a special point of emphasising that your company follows the highest ethical standards, which specifically prohibit under-the-table payments, and that you are bound by those standards. Anger or strong emotions should not be exhibited. You should apologise sincerely and stress that if you were to agree to any kind of unauthorised payment, you would be dismissed from your organisation. This point should only be mentioned if the Chinese official persists in indicating that a larger contribution is required in order to achieve a bureaucratic objective.

As a last resort, you should tell the Chinese official concerned that you are to meet with his or her superior for further discussions and that you are obliged, or indeed have been requested, to report all the problems you have encountered in China to the relevant department. This strategy should only be deployed if the official openly and continuously insists on the payment of a bribe. In cases where the corrupt individual continues to be uncooperative, it may help to discuss your problem, in private, with someone higher up in the chain of command. If the higher official agrees to grant the request, the subordinate must then act. This strategy should never be used as an open threat, since in China a humiliated official is likely to do their best to frustrate your every effort in the future.

Chapter 7

The Chinese Market and Consumer Psychology

China must be viewed as a growing and rapidly changing market full of business opportunities. Social mobility in China is faster than any Western country. Many large MNCs realise that they cannot ignore China, although presently sales for their particular brands are well below that of other markets. This chapter examines Chinese consumer behaviour, including complex questions of brand loyalty versus fashions or trends. This discussion is complicated by many social and cultural factors, which include the purchasing behaviours and tastes of a generation of upwardly mobile consumers who are much more open-minded than their more conservative elders. The emergence of a 'competitive purchase' psychology, questions of the relative social merits of saving prior to purchasing and budgeting, versus conspicuous consumption, is explained in the light of new patterns of consumer behaviour. Emerging market segments exhibit a strong desire to demonstrate wealth or status based on economic success and education as well as the traditional elements of family and *guanxi* relationships. This chapter addresses a wide range of market characteristics from the significance of the 'Golden Child' in family purchases, to the phenomenon of organisational purchases for non-productive purposes. These factors are explained in the context of China's complex market comprising over 50 ethnic groups, in a population of around 1.3 billion, scattered across an area of 9.6 million square kilometres.

China's average per capita urban net income was around US$759.00 for the year 2000, increasing by 5.7 per cent annually (Zhu, 2001). According to this index, China ranks economically in the middle of the world's less-developed countries, but remains poor by world standards generally. However, it is impossible to calculate the purchasing power of China's various consumer groups using average income as the sole guide. The Chinese market is very illusory. It is a market where the wealthy may 'spend gold on one throw' — for instance a business person may pay $1000 US dollars for one restaurant meal, whilst ordinary people are thrifty and count every cent towards a purchase.

In 1999 less than 5 percent of China's wealthy possessed half of all domestic savings, worth around 3000 billion RMB Yuan (Feng & Yen, 2001). Most importantly, the wealthy sector of Chinese society, which is most favourably inclined to high-quality products, especially foreign brands, is growing rapidly.

Consumer behavior

China is a rapidly industrialising society, which now produces a great deal of the world's capital goods and durable products. China's domestic brands have gradually begun to perform better in the market place. In accordance with the late Deng Xiao Ping's policy of "a portion of the population must become rich first", income disparity between social classes in Chinese society has become marked. This has had a profound impact on the Chinese market and on consumer psychology, for with the new found wealth there has also come an insatiable appetite for luxury goods and services.

Demographic Segmentation

Brand Loyalty versus Fashion Followers

Brand loyalty is predominantly a characteristic of the older generation of Chinese consumers. People aged over sixty years in China are unlikely to switch to other brands or products. They are more likely to believe that it is not worth the risk to abandon brand names that they have enjoyed for a long time. For them, trying new brands invites the possibility of a wrong purchase decision. The traditional values of 'a high avoidance of uncertainty' and maintaining a thrifty lifestyle continue to exert a strong influence on them. Their tendency to plan ahead for large purchases means that they prefer less expensive, familiar brands to a new brand selling at a higher price. The money saved on small, trusted items is put aside for larger, more expensive purchases. Older consumers make a purchase decision for expensive items relatively slowly and prudently. These age-linked demographic characteristics are even more striking when purchases of foreign brands are involved. Ordinary Chinese aged from fifty to over sixty years are conservative in their approach to foreign brands. Foreign and more expense brands are barely considered as an alternative to tried-and-tested local brands in the daily consumption patterns of this demographic group.

Compared with the older generation, younger, upwardly mobile consumers are much more open-minded about new brands, new products and new ideas. It is this group that now has the stronger purchasing power. China's youthful, post Open-Door generation is happy to accept anything new so long as it symbolises fashion, high social class or outstanding quality. Generally speaking, the tendency of this group to think ahead for large purchases is well known, as is their penchant for reasonably high-priced brands and products. The findings of a survey (Wang *et al*, 2000) indicate that the younger generation, living in urban areas, prioritises hedonistic values and tends to be more responsive to Western cultural influences and expensive foreign products or brands than older Chinese in rural areas. Clearly the younger generation in China has been influenced by Western tastes. They are the main consumer force behind the current purchase trend towards foreign brands with global standards and high prices. American cigarettes, German cars, Japanese electronic products, French cosmetics, British beer, Australian wine are all in fashion with China's new young rich. These products bestow credibility — they are symbols of fashion, good taste and wealth. The psychology of 'face' or status-related purchases strongly drives the younger generation to pursue these foreign goods. There are many cases where young people are bitterly criticised by the older generation for abandoning local brands for international choices. Flaunting these symbols tells the world that a particular consumer group is astute enough to recognise a trend, but in China, trends come at a price. Imported products are expensive when compared to most Chinese consumers' incomes. Nevertheless, young Chinese consumers are willing to pay for fashionable items in order to demonstrate their status. This is especially true of teenagers and young women.

Thanks to a broader range of choices, and a 'competitive purchase' psychology, many Chinese women are very concerned to keep abreast of the latest sartorial fashions. They are also keen to know which cosmetics are being used by the rich and famous and the latest body-care services that are coming on to the market. Unmarried women will not hesitate to spend most of their income on these goods and services, including a wide range of well-known foreign brands. They make quick purchasing decisions for expensive items and they pay for them in cash. For most Chinese women, in particular the younger generation, shopping in large department stores is one of the most pleasurable experiences of their lives. They browse the shelves and hunt for desirable products. Because of a general rise in the affluence of the entire country, consumers nowadays like to 'go shopping' and select from a wide range of products. Many stores have responded to this new demand by staying open until 10 p.m. seven nights a week.

The 'Golden Child' in Family Purchases

The child's role in family purchasing behaviour is now well recognised by marketing theorists around the world. Children are especially influential in how their parents make decisions regarding food, toys, clothing, vacations, recreation and automobiles (Lamb et al, 1996). This characteristic is fully evident in the Chinese market place, where it acquires added significance from the powerful influence of China's policy of one child per family. In the PRC, family expenditures — at least in urban areas — reveal the fact that the purchase of expensive goods, or even basic necessities, are dominated by needs and desires of the single child.

The Chinese government's population control program stipulates that families are only allowed to have one child. Currently, this policy is not well implemented in rural areas. However, due to the insistence of the government, and for economic reasons, this policy has been accepted by almost all young, urban-dwelling couples, especially in the large cities of Beijing, Shanghai and Guangzhou. Traditional Chinese culture, with its emphasis on the extended family structure (consisting of many relative adults and one child), have resulted in the child becoming the most privileged consumer in contemporary China.

The Chinese extended family, with its close relationships between generations, differs somewhat from the concept of family in many Western countries. The latter tend to be more oriented towards the nuclear family — a married couple and their pre-adult children. In China, the younger generation has a moral obligation to care for the elderly, especially when the latter becomes dependent because of old age or infirmity. In turn, parents have a moral and social obligation to care for their child for most of their lives. A very old Chinese saying maintains 'that if a son has not been properly educated or cultivated, then it is not his fault but the fault of his father'. Children in the West are expected to be independent after they reach the age of 18 years. In China, parents are expected to continue to support their children in most aspects of living and development long after they 'come of age'. Most Chinese parents dedicate their entire lives to supporting every aspect of their child's growth and development. Most Western parents, on the other hand, are grateful for the day their children 'leave the nest' and become independent adults.

The structure of the modern Chinese 'one-child family' reinforces this sense of parental obligation. The child is the focus of both the immediate and extended family. Because of this, Chinese parents are willing to suffer almost any hardship in order to make their child's life successful and comfortable. They will do their utmost to provide their child with the best education, the finest food, and the most modern clothes. For example, although the price of Beijing-produced milk is three times less expensive than the milk imported from Australia or Holland, the quality of imported milk is much better than that of the local product. Many parents in Beijing buy only imported Australian or Dutch milk for their child, though they themselves drink nothing but the local product (or even go without for the sake of their children).

Market research shows that Australian and Dutch milk products sell very well in the Beijing market because they are 'the best' and for Chinese parents nothing less will suffice for their 'golden child'.

Many young Chinese parents save for years after they first marry to buy a piano or other expensive musical instrument for their child. Music lessons can then begin before the child starts school. Early and intensive tuition is believed to give children a head start in the highly competitive Chinese school system. This involves costly private lessons that require disciplined saving on the part of parents. Expensive, but comprehensive, private instruction in the English language, computer studies, drawing, mathematics, and Mandarin calligraphy is also available. No expense, it seems, is too great for the present generation of urban 'golden children'.

In China most people know nothing about Mother's or Father's Day, but everyone knows that 1 June is International Child's Day. Parents, grandparents, friends, and school communities all celebrate this important day by holding elaborate ceremonies and lavishing gifts on their children. Similarly, on other important occasions, such as the traditional Chinese New Year, the child will often receive a generous allotment of pocket money from relatives or friends of their parents. This is because the giving of gifts is part of traditional Chinese festival culture, but also because the 'golden child' has become the focus of the entire family, even an entire community. Only child teenagers, have a constant opportunities to ask their parents to buy them well-known brands of footwear or clothing, despite the fact that these goods are usually much more expensive than the local product.

A survey conducted by the market-research firm AC Nielson (*Business China*, 2000), suggests that Chinese children are not more avid consumers than their counterparts in thirteen countries around the region. They rank a respectable 7th in terms of the amount of money they receive each year as gifts. The research also suggests that Chinese youth read more, study harder, and spend less time and money shopping than other Asian youths. However, the conclusions of this comparative study must be approached with some caution. Compared with Taiwan, Singapore and Hong Kong, the average child's standard of living in China today is lower. Although in purely numerical terms, the number of affluent children in China is much greater than in Taiwan or Singapore.

Wealthy children are at the highest levels of consumption, with their consumer needs always placed at the top of the family list. This group keeps increasing with the growth of the China economy. It is reported (*Heilong-Jiang Daily*, 2001) that Chinese university students in Hailong Jiang province (one of less developed regions in China), spend the greatest proportion of their total expenditure on travelling, computers, mobile phones, pagers and entertainment. Moreover good proportion of students purchase foreign brands when it comes to buying clothes, cosmetics and footwear. Family financial support is the main source of income for 92.7 per cent of university students living on campus. According to the report, students in the highest expenditure level spent up to 18, 000 RMB annually.

In urban areas, most families hope that their only child will go to university or achieve a higher degree because levels of income and social status are increasingly being linked to academic qualifications in modern China, a trend which in turn is supported by both current recruitment criteria and contemporary cultural expectations. A family's 'central policy', therefore, is to meet all the needs of their child, which includes doing everything they can to help them to gain entrance into the best schools and universities. As a result, children's consumer goods, ranging from exotic and nutritional foods to 'study aids' (which are supposed to develop intelligence), all sell extremely well in the Chinese market.

Socio-Economic Segmentation

The growth of purchasing power is an indication that in China the average income has increased. Under the transitional economy, a modern Chinese market place is emerging, but it is still immature, with fragmented market segmentations. One can argue that changes in the Chinese market are too dramatic to be fully reflected in contemporary academic journals. However the main direction of Chinese society is towards general prosperity. Ordinary people's salaries have in fact risen ten to fifteen times within the last twenty years, while people involved in commercial activities have seen an even more dramatic increase in their incomes. Social mobility in China is in fact faster than any Western country.

Extravagance versus Thrift

The rapid rise of certain income groups has produced a 'wealth gap' while levels of purchasing power have become unpredictable. These changes have had a profound impact on the Chinese market and consumer behaviour. Currently, China's salaried classes acquire their income from three main sources. The first is a person's formal salary and associated subsidies. In the case of SOEs, salaries are nationally standardised according to each industry, while subsidies or fringe benefits are dependent on the specific policies of the organisation that he or she works for. In China, a poorly performing enterprise may not be able to issue subsidies to its employees, while a profitable organisation may issue a subsidy higher than the formal salary. People who work in private companies can also expect an income that is higher than the national average. Senior managers working for foreign companies and joint ventures, and project contractors, popular actors, and members of the medical profession, are paid the highest salaries of all.

A second source of remuneration in contemporary China is referred to as 'grey income'. These are wages derived from informal or concurrent work. For example, manufacturing workers may run street stalls to boost their income or take night jobs after normal working hours. This group also includes university academics who provide consultancy or training programs to business, and enterprise managers who may hold simultaneous appointments with different organisations.

A third source of income is 'black income'. This is acquired from illegal, corrupt or immoral activities. For example, a government official may obtain a 'back-hander' or a commission for speeding-up the bureaucratic process, or a doctor may receive an extra payment in return for offering better treatment or responding to a case more promptly.

The owners of private companies — even quite small businesses — are beginning to make solid profits from their commercial activities. The Chinese magazine *Reform* (no.2, 1995) reported that there were over 2 million millionaires in China. Thus, in the PRC there are people who are only earning 300 RMB yuan a month (about $US36), while others may be taking home 20,000 RMB *yuan* a month (about $US2418).

Because of this disparity in incomes, a very wide range of goods can be sold successfully in the Chinese market. Although there are many who have to budget diligently for every major purchase, there are others who can afford to buy whatever they like. The Chinese population is predominantly composed of the former, who carefully consider whether the price and quality of a product is reasonable before making a purchase. The most famous and exclusive imported brands in the world have loyal customers in China, as do some low-priced, reasonable-quality, imported goods.

Socio-Economic Pyramid

The increase in the average level of incomes in China has not been accompanied by a commensurate growth in the middle class. A pyramid-shaped social framework represents the characteristics of income in China with the lower class constituting the majority. A survey conducted in 1997 indicates that Chinese consumers in urban areas fall into four major socio-economic categories. Cui and Liu (2001) label them the Rich, 'Yuppies', the Salary Class, and the Working Class Poor, with the latter constituting the majority. These divisions are reasonable, but the labels and definitions that underpin them are questionable. One of the obvious reasons for this is that many working class poor of the fourth rank are also salary earners, as are the third rank by definition, and that they themselves are upwardly socially mobile.

Based on income rankings, the Chinese population can be divided into working class poor, lower-middle class, middle class and upper-class wealthy. Poor-performance urbanites, relying on basic salaries, constitute a part of the working class poor, but rural peasants make up the larger portion of this class. They are the 'strugglers' — the people with the least purchasing power, who cannot afford to buy global standardised brands.

People who work in government organisations, which have been able to maintain a reasonable commercial performance, can expect certain fringe benefits, such as housing, medical care, and so on.

This group is mostly comprised of the numerically smaller lower-middle class. Although they spend nearly half their wages on food and other necessities, they are likely to buy the occasional luxury item, such as air-conditioners, computers, DVDs and so on.

At the top end of the normal salary range, there are people who are able to earn extra money from 'grey' or 'black' incomes because of their special skills, expertise, knowledge or even exclusive authority. They comprise, for the most part, the Chinese middle class. This class also includes the employees of state-owned enterprises, as well as those who work for higher-performing local and foreign private companies. For some senior managers in this group, easy access to organisational funds enables them to spend money which is not strictly theirs. They may not be able to afford many luxury items, but buying some luxury goods, especially those of foreign manufacture, is a popular way of demonstrating their social status and is definitely within the range of their consumption pattern.

Entrepreneurs, businesspeople, celebrities and the owners of private companies comprise the upper-middle class wealthy. The size of this group is very limited and its members earn a much higher income than the average Chinese household. They are mainly aged between thirty to forty years, with 37 per cent between forty and fifty years (*China Information Daily*, 2001). They can afford the entire range of social and material attributes associated with wealth and buy luxury or foreign-brand products. Many upper-class Chinese have cars, travel overseas and develop sophisticated tastes. The number of Chinese citizens in this class has been increasing steadily since the mid-1990s.

Organisational Segmentation
Purchases for Non-productive Purposes
There are two types of organisational purchase in China. The first

is when an organisation makes purchases to operate their business. This is just like anywhere else in the world. The other type is to purchase non-productive consumer goods such as food, disposable commodities, houses, entertainment or holiday vouchers for employees. As described in Chapter Five, a Chinese enterprise is like a small society with its own collective identity and mutual obligations. Management is responsible for both the private and working lives of its employees. This includes taking care of employees' welfare by arranging and buying all manner of goods, especially for important events.

Non-productive organisational purchases may also include gifts, the cost of luxury hotel accommodation, overseas trips, banquets and all the other expenditures that serve to promote the organisation's commercial interests in the Chinese business community. For example, a company may buy an entertainment package for its business partners or official supporters.

Non-productive organisational purchases are a general market phenomenon in China and large sums are spent this way. A survey conducted by Chinese marketing statisticians found that nearly one third of all consumer goods in the Chinese market place were bought in this way in 1998. For this reason, an effective means of suppressing inflation is to limit non-productive organisation purchases by administrative means. For instance, the government issued a directive whereby any purchase of a particular non-productive item must first be approved by the relevant governmental department.

Geographic Segmentation

Regional Diversity: 'Four Economic Worlds'

China is a conglomeration of fragmented markets divided by variations in economic development, industrial preferences and local cultures. China has over 50 ethnic groups, in a population of around 1.3 billion, which is scattered across an area of 9.6 million square kilometres. A great range of topographical and climatic conditions have had a tremendous impact on Chinese people's lifestyles and economic development. Even the majority Han people, who comprise some 91.3 per cent of the total population, do not have a homogeneous culture, but are diversified by dialect, subculture and lifestyle across many different regions. Market research suggests that regional differences in economic, cultural and consumer characteristics have resulted in the evolution of very distinctive markets, which can be classified in terms of their economic development (Zikmund, and D'amico, 1996).

Hu (2001), a Chinese economist, argues that China is being divided into 'four economic worlds' in terms of purchasing-power-parity (PPP), with exchange rates adjusted to offset different inflation rates. A few large cities located in China's coastal areas including Beijing, Shanghai, Guangzhou and Shengzhen have the highest PPP in China. Shanghai, for example, is US$ 15,516 and Beijing is US$ 9,916. These cities are the most advanced in terms of economic infrastructure and market development. They can be described as 'first world' and are the cities most targeted by MNCs.

Among the second rank cities and provinces, Tianjin, Guangdong, Zhejang, Jiangsun, Fujian and Liaoning come out on top with a PPP of US$ 3,960. This group is also coastal but they are less developed than the premier cities of Beijing, Shenjian and Shanghai and the others. They are referred to as 'second world'.

Cities in the Northeast and the North of China, such as those in Hebei Province, are ranked as 'third world', with an average PPP below cities of comparable size and complexity in other parts of the world. Finally, there are the relatively poor and backward provinces of North- and Southwest China, which include Inner Mongolia, Shanxi, Gausu, Guizhou, Yuan and Guangxi. These are the least developed territories in China, with a PPP of US$ 1,247 or less, and are identified by Hu as belonging to the 'fourth world'.

City Diversity

People often think of China as being divided into two parts — Northern China and Southern China — with the Yangtze River constituting a kind of border separating the two regions. There are obvious differences between consumer habits in the north and those in the south. Generally speaking, the consumers of large cities in southern China, like Shanghai and Hangzhou, are more careful about calculating the value of their purchases. They are also more likely to budget for goods than are consumers in North China. They are more likely to carefully compare the price and quality of goods and services before making a purchase decision. The southern Chinese understand and follow fashion and generally select goods that are appropriate to their social class or profession. They are well known for their sophisticated tastes in relation to both domestic and international brands.

In contrast, consumers in the large cities of northern China, such as Harbin and Shangyong spend their money more freely and generously, though the average income of people in the north of China is actually less than that of Southerners. The economic imbalance between North and South is primarily due to developmental differences in the regional economies. However, the purchasing power of northern consumers is no less than in the South. Indeed, consumer purchasing power for high-fashion clothing and cosmetics in North China is even stronger than in some cities of the South. Moreover, compared to people living south of the Yangtze

River, Northerners are much less likely to compare the price or quality of goods and services before making a purchase decision.

The Psychology of Chinese Consumers

Relating Chinese cultural values to purchase psychology can provide interesting insights into the behaviour of Chinese consumers. There are four outstanding characteristics that define Chinese consumer psychology and they ultimately derive from the peculiarities of Chinese culture.

Saving Prior to Consuming

Consumer behaviour in many Western countries indicates that consumption patterns are linked to 'present and future income'. People who purchase goods, especially prior to Christmas, often use credit cards or some other form of deferred payment. They accept the fact that they have to pay a higher interest rate for this service. They believe that improving the immediate quality of their lives justifies their overspending patterns in the long term.

In contrast, Chinese customers insist that consumption must be based on 'past saving' and 'current income'. In their mind, money should be used either for necessity or for generating a return. Any expenditure that involves 'extra' costs (such as interest payments), and which requires the consumer to borrow money, is considered unwise and best avoided. Chinese customers prefer to save their money and then pay in full. For example, a Chinese consumer will typically purchase furnishings worth US$2000 by paying cash after a long period of saving, while a Westerner will typically pay by instalment or by credit. Significantly, the cost of the goods may constitute six months wages for a Chinese factory worker but only two weeks for a Westerner.

The rate of personal savings in China is high compared with many other countries. China's national domestic savings reached US$ 767.74 billion up to November 2000. A survey conducted in China's five largest cities — Beijing, Chongqing, Guangzhou, Shenyang and Shanghai revealed that 48 per cent of families held average savings of over 10,000 RMB *yuan* (about $US1209) in 1997. In short, Chinese people avoid spending money on medium or large purchases without first having planned and then saved for it.

Chinese people also practice 'saving for a rainy day'. The success of American Assurance (AAA) in China and among overseas Chinese illustrates this. Life and medical insurance for Westerners in developed countries is based on consumption, and typically comprises small but regular payments towards the financial recovery of clients in the event of an incident or accident requiring a benefit. However, as is the case with insurance policies everywhere, clients may not benefit at all from their insurance if there is no qualifying event or accident.

This concept is not accepted by many Chinese. On the other hand, Chinese consumers are happier to be involved in investment schemes, as a form of life insurance, which can be used for both *saving* and *gaining* interest. AAA founded its business in Shanghai over 50 years ago and has been continually attracting Chinese customers in many countries by applying this psychology in their strategic marketing plan. Under *saving* and *gaining* schemes especially set up for the Chinese market, Chinese policy holders can claim all investments in life insurance back, plus interest, after a certain number of years.

Chinese consumers are not accustomed to applying for credit when buying goods. Nowadays, a small number of Chinese consumers will apply for a loan if they want to buy a car or a house, but this is a relatively recent development. China's banks did not offer loans for the purchase of any private purpose, durable commodity until the early 1990s. Even now, because of the continued banking restrictions in China, most ordinary salary earners are not eligible for bank loans.

The Chinese values of 'face protection' and 'avoidance of uncertainty' cultivates this particular feature of Chinese consumer psychology. For instance, if a Chinese person borrows money to buy a television set, his friends and relatives will consider him both foolish and a poor manager of his personal finances. For most Chinese consumers, the act of purchasing is not just a simple transaction. It demonstrates an individual's financial capacity and social status. This in turn serves to meet the individuals' psychological need for social esteem.

As mentioned in Chapter Two, the Chinese people are group oriented and like to maintain close relationships within their respective communities. There is no clear distinction between public and private life in China and people within a particular community or network involve themselves in most aspects of each other's daily lives. An application to borrow money is generally understood by the community in two ways: that the applicant did not have the sufficient earning capacity to purchase the goods in the first place, or alternately, that the person did not have the self control to save. Many Chinese people believe that borrowing money to buy goods is a form of public embarrassment. It causes them to 'lose face' with their contemporaries.

Another reason is that borrowing money from others in China has traditionally been seen as a risky activity. Most ordinary Chinese would feel more comfortable in waiting a little longer and saving a little harder in order to be able to pay cash for their purchases. These cultural values, together with the realities of the present banking system in China, all reinforce the habit of 'saving prior to consuming'. This profoundly influences the buying behaviour of the majority of Chinese consumers.

Vying for Purchasing

The outstanding characteristic of Chinese consumer behaviour is of 'vying with others for the glory of purchasing'. The buying behaviour of most Chinese people is strongly influenced by a number of reference groups. These groups generate a strong desire to buy relatively expensive items, especially when a particular item has become popular or has already been bought by relatives, friends or neighbours. Some people, who cannot afford to buy a popular product immediately, may be driven 'half mad' by 'vying psychology' and will concentrate all their efforts on saving up for it. They will even reduce their spending on the necessities of daily life for a short period in order to save for this particular purpose.

Because of the closeness of group members within the Chinese community, the popularity of a given product may increase rapidly. Chinese consumers are more likely to accept a product if product information is spread through both informal and personal channels as well as formal or official channels of communication.

This 'vying for purchasing' mentality is closely connected to the Chinese idea of 'absolute egalitarianism'. The latter value not only influences people's views about wealth allocation, but also has an impact on their buying behaviour. Most ordinary people in China believe that there should not be an excessive disparity of wealth or standard of living between people within the same social class. One would feel 'a loss of face', if one could not afford to purchase an expensive item, especially if it was an item that was already currently available to others within the same social class.

Often Chinese consumers will all at once rush to purchase the same kinds of goods and services at a particular moment in time. The habit of saving prior to consuming provides the financial and psychological basis for 'vying for purchasing'. Ordinary people always have money put away for such 'necessities'. The psychology of both vying for purchasing and saving prior to consuming shapes the Chinese market. Chinese consumers with low average incomes may be able afford to buy relatively expensive goods in sizeable volumes.

Case Study: A Winning Strategy

In the late 1970s, several Japanese and Western electronic companies conducted market research into the Chinese purchasing power of household electrical goods. Western companies decided that the Chinese market was not ready for such products, as China's per capital GDP was only around US$300. Based on their own experience of Western markets, it was believed that per capital GDP of US$1000 or over was required before consumers were ready to buy household electrical goods. Japanese companies took a completely different view, although they were working with similar market research data. They understood that firstly, Chinese consumers' psychology of saving prior to consuming would make them want to buy these preferred expensive purchases. Secondly, China's huge population meant that even if only a very low percentage of the total number of consumers could actually afford to buy electronic goods, this still represented a reasonable market — in this instance, a niche market is in fact a mass market. Thirdly, Chinese consumer psychology of 'vying purchasing' guaranteed the growth of electrical goods sales in the long run. In addition, the Japanese also predicted that the sales of electrical goods would be stimulated by China's Open Door policy, which made it much easier for overseas Chinese to visit their homeland — they guessed, correctly, that the visitors from overseas would introduce their mainland relatives to the desirability of electronic household appliances. Accordingly, the Japanese companies set up a marketing strategy based on these considerations and successfully seized a sizeable share of China's electrical products market at that time.

Understanding Chinese consumer psychology made all the difference in terms of the early success of these Japanese companies in the Chinese market. The important difference was that the Western companies based their strategies on certain 'beliefs' about the Chinese market whereas the Japanese companies based their strategies on knowledge and cultural insight. For Westerners, China is a place of which 'much is believed but little is known'.

Relationship Driven Purchasing

In the Chinese market, there are many occasions that require gift-giving. These include 1) 'face enhancement', 2) interpersonal relationship building and 3) building *guanxi* networks. As established, many Chinese consumers possess strong motives to buy luxury goods, not for personal consumption, but as gifts for others. People in low-income groups might never dream of actually buying the same goods for themselves, as such items would ordinarily be well beyond their means. While gift-giving has been covered at length in Chapter Six, it bears reconsideration in the light of consumer behaviour.

The purpose of gift-giving generosity, is to strengthen a wide range of mutually beneficial interpersonal relationships. Sometimes it is simply a matter of courtesy. For example, a valuable gift is often presented to one's 'boss' before or after one receives a pay rise or promotion, A special token of appreciation may be presented to the principal of a good school for processing a child's enrolment. A gift may be lovingly presented to the aged in order to demonstrate filial piety; to a teacher for his or her special help with a child's study; to a doctor for providing immediate and expert treatment; or to a director of a housing committee for obtaining an accommodation allocation. In considering these various interactions, the giver must select the 'right' gift for the 'right' person and occasion. The receiver's gender, likes, needs, social status and relative personal and professional value must be taken into account. The right time can be anytime during a special occasion, festival or public holiday. These are all seen as good opportunities for establishing or strengthening relationships.

In business, people believe that buying appropriate gifts presents the best opportunity to show their respect or financial strength to the receiver, or to attract their favourable attention. Expensive, exotic or unique goods are especially chosen as gifts for businesspeople. On festive occasions, imported wines, flowers, expensive European wrist watches or exotic imported handicrafts are popular options as are clothes, nutritional or novelty foods, fine linen as well as electronic items such as television sets. This universal custom of gift-giving drives Chinese consumers' expenditure over their necessary spending on daily life and increases their purchasing desires.

Flaunting Consumption

Flaunting consumption occurs when consumers intend to publicly demonstrate their wealth or status. As mentioned above, for most Chinese consumers the act of purchasing is not a simple monetary transaction. It is related to a demonstration of an individual's financial capacity and social status. For ordinary people, this psychology is represented through vying purchasing, where the intent is to maintain one's social status with others. Amongst the rich, the motivation may be to flaunt their privileged position in the Chinese economy and enhance their social status. In the view of many Chinese people, 'face' and social status are the most important matters in life. Luxury goods are symbols that publicly demonstrate status. This is a common belief in all Chinese societies including both Mainland and overseas Chinese communities.

In China today, flaunting consumption is limited to a few small but influential groups. These groups are mainly composed of wealthy businesspeople, young professionals and youths in urban areas, and the senior managers of state- and collective-owned enterprises who have access to the expense accounts of their organisations. Although these consumers are small in number, their purchasing power is huge. They prefer to buy high-quality, popular and expensive products in order to show their outstanding financial status. That is why some well-known global brands with a very high price — even higher than in the markets of developed countries — can sell well in China's large capital cities. The group is composed of youths or young adults in urban areas who either receive financial support from their wealthy families or earn high incomes with their skills and knowledge. This group often pursues prestigious brand names to flaunt their status and enhance their 'face'. This group has also developed sophisticated tastes and often chooses good brands based on their reliability, price and because they have a long-established reputation for quality or performance. However, as Cui and Lui (2001) have indicated, they may not always opt for foreign brands at a higher price. Instead, they may go for well-known, high-quality domestic brands at a lower price, since some Chinese manufacturers have closed the quality gap with their foreign competitors.

The reforms of 1978 have enabled many Chinese businessmen and women to become millionaires. Many of these very wealthy people are not formally educated. Some have very humble backgrounds indeed, having risen from the lowest social strata of Chinese society. Because China is a society that combines the traditional values of hierarchy with a modern respect for intelligence, there is little true respect for those wealthy 'upstarts' with little intellectual or cultural sophistication. In spite of a great deal of money, the status of some members of China's wealthiest class remains quite low. These wealthy people will often attempt to use their money to 'buy' a form of status or reputation in society. In doing so, they will try almost anything to meet their need to achieve social esteem or 'face'.

Case Study: Can Status be Purchased?

One day in 1990, a resident who appeared to be a simple peasant walked into a five-star hotel located in the Beijing CBD. The man wanted to enquire about accommodation. The receptionist informed the man that this particular hotel was not an appropriate place for him to stay. The receptionist's condescending manner enraged the peasant who felt an acute 'loss of face'. He continually asked her about the cost of the room. The receptionist replied, "Why do you ask this question as clearly you can not afford even a fraction of the nightly tariff"? This time the man lost his temper completely because there were many people in the hotel lobby watching the spectacle. The man retorted, "I will stay in no place other than in the best room in this hotel". "The best room costs US$1200 a night", the receptionist answered. The man sarcastically replied, "Only US$1200. I would pay US$2200 if necessary". The man then paid the appropriate tariff to stay in the hotel's VIP suite, though he needed a great deal of assistance to complete his registration form. The man's response was typical of the show-off behaviour adopted by many of China's new rich.

Nightclubs in China's large cities are the main public forums for this type of showing off. In these places guests sit together to talk and drink a great deal of expensive, imported spirits. Often brands will be cost over US$200 a bottle. The more expensive and exclusive the brand, the more important it is to be seen drinking it. Sometimes if one patron has paid US$50 to one of the nightclub entertainers to sing a particular song, another person may offer to pay US$100 for the same singer to sing the same song. The tune will then be performed and dedicated to the highest bidder. The expenses of any one of these customers will often exceed several months' salary for an ordinary worker. Although the average Chinese consumer condemns this behaviour and the Chinese government strongly discourages 'non-thrifty conduct', showing off consumer behaviour can be seen everywhere in China. Because of this service industries are booming across China, as are sales of imported luxury alcoholic drinks.

Chapter 8

Effective Marketing

Effective promotion and distribution of goods and services make the difference between market penetration and anonymity. It is therefore an essential ingredient to any successful sales strategy. This chapter begins with a marketing research overview. It examines the skills and strategies of promotion in branding, as well as packaging and advertising, as seen from a Chinese cultural perspective. Ignoring factors such as culturally appropriate brand building and evaluation means courting unacceptable risk. To reduce business risks to the lowest degree possible, we strongly suggest that comprehensive and effective market research is necessary before a foreign firm enters China. How to differentiate the various media within a sophisticated network of governmental control and to work with these media for different segments of the Chinese market is also explained. The role of public relations in promotion is discussed at length. This section includes a careful differentiation of the advantages of working with media administrated by the central government, by provincial and municipal governments, by country governments and by large state-owned enterprises. This section also includes up-to-date information about Internet use in China where in late 2002 dial-up connections numbered 15.43 million subscribers. Finally we examine advertising strategies and the role of public relations in promotion, including publicity-orientated, socially oriented, consultative and public-good-oriented public relations.

Market Research
Knowing the Market

"For a foreign company entering China, accurate market research is critical: Whether you are selling soap or cell-phones, insights into where, when, and how to launch your product can make the difference between early success and costly failure" (Slater, 1999: 66)

With 1.3 billion consumers, the market in the PRC has huge consumer demand. China has a number of unique and exploitable consumer characteristics, existing in a relatively independent market. The latter is in the process of being transformed from an immature, centrally-planned monolith into a dynamic, market-orientated system. All these factors combine to make current and accurate commercial information the life-blood of the Chinese market. To reduce business risks to the lowest degree possible, comprehensive and effective market research is necessary before a foreign firm contemplates entering China.

Obtaining relevant commercial data in China is difficult. First, there is the problem of diverse ownership. This often leads to enormous differences in pricing and marketing channels (local protectionism) among state-owned and other types of enterprises. It also makes it difficult to comprehend the overall situation concerning marketing development. In contrast to developed countries in the West, where enterprise data is widely available, less than 20 per cent of all Chinese enterprises make such data available to the public or to relevant industry groups. Sales volumes, market shares, company finance and so on, are important statistics that should appear in an annual report for the scrutiny of investors, but both the Chinese government and most state-owned organisations traditionally regard business information as state secrets to be protected at all cost. The Chinese government supervises all large-scale surveys in order to avoid leaks of sensitive information. A strict regulation, introduced in China in 1999, is that any focus group targeted for market research or large-scale survey has to receive prior approval from the State Statistical Bureau and that the findings must also be reviewed by the Bureau before the client sees the results for themselves.

Another problem is that the accounting systems of many Chinese companies have not been completely standardised in terms of international conventions, chiefly because international accounting standards were not introduced into China until the early 1990s. As a result, some accountants still do not hold formal qualifications. Accounting data may not accurately reflect a particular firm's real financial situation and may therefore be of little use to marketers or investors.

Chinese consumers face accelerating change in most areas of their lives. The introduction of new products and new ways of retailing, set against a backdrop of increased incomes, is constantly changing Chinese consumer values and behaviour. This means that any data about the Chinese market becomes obsolete very quickly. The complication of disparate pricing and distribution systems, the lack of publicly available commercial data, an undeveloped accounting system and changing consumer values all result in a situation where it is difficult to predict the Chinese market. It is essential that any foreign company planning to enter the Chinese market should hire professional Chinese marketing researchers to assist them in this matter.

Before the reforms of 1978 the State Statistics Bureau collected and controlled most data about the Chinese market. Private market research companies in China did not appear until the late 1980s. Although there are currently many regional marketing consultative companies in China, only a few of them have the capacity to conduct nationwide surveys and provide a standardised research report. One of exceptions is Beijing's Huiecong International. This company is the largest private, professional marketing research company in China, with over forty subsidiaries and 1800 staff operating nationwide. The Huiecong Group International has developed a vast database which incorporates product quotation and marketing research with a comprehensive monitoring system. The Huiecong Group's international customers include many well-known companies such as IBM, Intel, Epson, APC, Philips, Farstar and Hewlett Packard.

Organising Market Research

Choosing a good market research organisation is a crucial first step. The market research company of choice should have a high profile and possess a nationwide network. Ideally it should have extensive experience in conducting surveys on behalf of multinational enterprises. Foreign clients should ask the selected company to provide a detailed proposal and fee schedule, for although consultancy proposals may be free in the West, in China a fee is charged. The foreign company must then sign an agreement with the Chinese consultative company to ensure that key goals are met. The terms of agreement usually include research objectives, project scope and schedule, content of the report, cost and payment options, copyright, arbitration and confidentiality. Quality control of research methods and data, as well as standards of translation, also need to be predetermined and incorporated into the contract. This is especially important if the foreign company requires a time limitation on research and a final report in English. Large marketing research companies like the Huiecong International Group are able to provide all of the above as well as the following international-standard, professional consultancy services:

- General market reports — this service covers sales volume, or the number of retailers and wholesalers for a certain product
- Sale ranking and research of best-sellers, market analysis and product forecasts
- Analysis of the market structure according to specified dimensions, including trade structure, market share, or technological specifications
- Analysis of the distribution of a particular brand or type of product
- Analysis of brand price and/or profits
- Analysis of product end-users
- Analysis of the appearance rate of advertisements
- Analysis of the market investment environment

Sales Promotion
Branding
Branding plays a very powerful role in the promotion of goods and services in the Chinese market. Most Chinese consumers are truly brand-guided. The difference between consumer groups in China is that older consumers are more likely to be loyal to certain brands, while middle-aged or younger consumers are more likely to pursue well-known, new or popular brands. Again, to Chinese consumers,

well-known brands not only mean quality but also represent either financial or social status. A comparison of the respective views of Chinese and Japanese consumers clearly indicates that Chinese consumers are more brand-driven and susceptible to fashion than their Japanese counterparts (Xue, 2000 in Table 8.1). Many multinational corporations make use of this knowledge to successfully gain a market share by merging their brands with local brands in the Chinese market place.

Table 8.1 A Comparison of Chinese and Japanese Consumers on Consumption Views

Item	Chinese (%)	Japanese (%)
1. Thrifty purchases	69	67
2. Preference for well-known brands	28	11
3. Should compare prior to purchase	69	64
4. Buy preferred goods, even on a tight budget.	45	20
5. Desire for something conspicuous	23	10
6. Desire to purchase what others have	22	7

Source: International Advertising, 1998 (Xue, 2000)

In principle, brand names should be easy to remember, and easy to pronounce. They should invoke a positive connotation and image, and reinforce both the international appeal and benefits of the product.

Some successful branding strategies used by local companies and MNCs in the Chinese market include:

1. Promote sub-brand names under a main, well-known brand in order to attract a wider group of consumers and meet the needs of a larger range of consumers.

2. Associate high technology with the brand from a functional perspective.
3. Associate high quality of product and services with the brand.
4. Associate symbols of high status with the brand.

One should note here that although a brand name in China plays the same promotional role as in other countries, it does so in a different way. In the West, people pay much more attention to how a brand name *sounds* when it is read aloud. The Chinese, on the other hand, place a great deal of emphasis on the *meaning* of a brand word and pay much more attention to its positive connotation and associated benefits. A baby boy in China may be given a name 'Bowen', which means that his parents hope that he will grow up to be knowledgeable in literature. A baby girl may be given a name 'Lingyu', which means that her parents wish her to be clever and beautiful. The same principle is true for choosing a brand name in Chinese business culture.

Chinese consumers usually make a brand decision according to both the meaning and the sound of a particular word, but meaning is thought to be more important than the sound on most occasions. The meaning of a brand name must be considered from two perspectives. The first is to attempt to directly tell the consumer how good the product is, or to inform them of the functions or advantages of selecting this particular brand. For example, Chinese consumers have favourably responded to a brand of detergent called 'Yixiling'. Yixiling means, ' clothes are made clean immediately when being touched by this particular brand of detergent'.

Another perspective on how and why a particular brand name is chosen is that a given brand may indicate that the product will bring the consumer a 'lucky result', 'good fortune,' 'high status' or 'best wishes'. For example, a brand of soap especially produced for older people is given the name 'Zitian', which in Mandarin Chinese means 'purple sandalwood'. In Chinese culture 'purple sandalwood' carries a very positive implicit meaning, namely that old people are valued members of society. This is because many Chinese believe that the older a purple sandalwood plant is, the stronger its fragrance.

Similarly, an expensive brand of men's shirts is called 'Sheng-Shi' meaning 'gentleman'. This brand's image implies a man who would wear such a shirt is characterised by dignity and sophistication. This brand sells very well not just because it is a high-quality article, but also because Chinese consumers feel very warm towards the actually brand name meaning.

There are some imported goods which have attractive sounding brand names in terms of the language of the brand's country of origin, but are practically meaningless to a Chinese consumer. To counter this , Chinese marketers often attempt to confer a Chinese meaning onto the similar sound of a particular foreign brand so that it can be understood and accepted by Chinese consumers without a significant sound change. In practice, the translation of foreign brand names into Chinese can be flexible according to either the sound or meaning of the original brand name. A successful principle of a brand translation is to combine the original sound with a meaningful connotation. For example, the soft-drink product, Sprite, produced by the Coca-Cola Company, is translated into Chinese as 'Xuebi' on the basis that the word sounds a bit like Spirit, rather than being a literal translation of the word 'sprite' into Chinese. The word *xuebi* in Chinese indicates a beautiful snowy scene filled with pristine ice crystals. This is intended to stimulate the Chinese consumers to imagine the drink making people feel cool and comfortable in hot weather. Chinese marketers carefully chose a new name with a similar sound, but with a special meaning that is attractive to Chinese consumers. Similarly, the brand name Coca Cola is translated as *Kekou-Kele*, which means that the product is tasty and enjoyable. A brand of Swiss wristwatch called Rado is translated as Leida, not only because the sound of the word is like that of the original brand name, but also because *leida* means 'radar', which is intended to convince Chinese consumers that this brand of watch is extremely accurate.

In the light of Chinese cultural sensitivities, there are a number of branding principles that provide a reference point for the design of appropriate and successful brand names. A brand intended for use by the older generation should relate to a meaning that indicates a particular health benefit. An appropriate brand name for a child's product should relate to intelligence or well being. For men, the best brand should suggest a sense of blessing, good luck, high status, financial success or business acumen. For women, the most successful brand names are connected with beauty.

Packaging

The important functions of packaging are to contain and protect the product, to promote the contents, and to facilitate storage for ease of delivery and finally for use. Of these, promotion is now the most important packaging function in China. Design, colours, shapes, and packaging materials all have a powerful impact on consumers' perceptions and buying behaviour. This function has, in the past, been ignored by Chinese manufacturers.

In the planned economy that existed before 1978, Chinese enterprises paid little attention to packaging aesthetics. Nor had they any interest in finding out the consumers' point of view.

Most product packaging was either dated or unfashionable compared to contemporary packaging in the West. Often the packaging was just plain ugly. This weakened the competitive advantage of some Chinese products in both the domestic and international market. After the implementation of the Open Door policy, changes in consumers' basic requirements, combined with market competition, forced Chinese enterprises to pay attention to packaging. Foreign products featuring novel or elegant packaging provided a reference point for Chinese manufacturers, particularly after the 1980s when foreign goods poured into the Chinese market.

These influences have completely changed the way products are presented for sale in China. Chinese consumers' packaging requirements are now very high, especially because of the custom of gift-giving, which demands that goods must appear both beautiful and valuable. Since in China it is not appropriate to open a gift in public, the gift-giver must ensure that the packaging accurately reflects the contents, so that everyone who witnesses the presentation will be impressed. The primary social function of packaging is to give the receiver 'face', and in return the gift-giver also gains 'face'. Chinese consumers are therefore willing to pay a high price for a product with elegant packaging. There have been many examples in the Chinese market where the sales of a particular product have increased dramatically after being presented in a more attractive manner or specifically designed as a gift package. When there are two rival brands of the same quality, the one with the most impressive packaging will command the higher price and the higher sales volume in the Chinese market. A product with an intrinsically high value will hardly be recognised by Chinese customers if its packaging design style looks plain. Foreign companies who wish to sell their products in China must pay careful attention to this.

Case Study: Wine

Two vintages of imported wine appeared in the Beijing market in 1995. One was produced in Australia, the other in France. Many Chinese consumers were aware that both France and Australia were two of the most famous wine-producing countries in the world. However, respective sales of the two vintages were significantly different. The French wine outsold the Australian wine by many times. In terms of price there was not much difference between the two competitors, but their packaging was different. The former was packed in a slender and refined spruce wood box, with a judicious amount of red ribbon and gold leaf. This looked both notable and grand, and conveyed the impression that the contents were at least as good as the packaging. This brand became both popular and famous. Beijing consumers quickly fell in love with this particular wine, and it remained the market leader for many years. One important reason for this success was that Chinese consumers regarded the French wine as one of the most impressive options for gift-giving because it was so beautifully presented. The Australian wine was of a similar, or even higher standard, but the way it was presented was ordinary, even pedestrian. It attracted very little attention and was overlooked by Chinese consumers. The Australian wine was marketed in single unpackaged bottles, unlike its elaborately boxed French competitor. One reason for the French success in this market was that they were astute enough to take expert advice from a specialist in marketing to the Chinese. The Australians felt that the quality of their wine would speak for itself. In the end the Chinese consumers made their choice and the French product prevailed. Consumption of table wine took off in the early 1990s in China when the health aspects of drinking wine were promoted. Chinese consumers mainly drink medium quality, low priced, locally-made wine on a daily basis. Under normal circumstances, ordinary consumers are not willing to spend very much on expensive goods for their own consumption, but feel that it is worth paying extra to successfully fulfil the social requirements of gift-giving or when hosting important banquets. For Chinese consumers, wine, or indeed any other alcoholic drink that is not packaged in an elaborate box, festooned with lace, ribbon and gold paint is unsuitable as a gift. The Australian wine marketers did not correctly identify a market position for their product and were too concerned to keep their costs and price down by avoiding elegant packing. Their wine came in plain bottles, but sold at a higher price compared to locally-produced wines. In opting for this sales strategy, they ignored the facts that in China, people are willing to pay extra money for products that can serve social networking needs. As a result Australian wines did not compete well with French wines in the Beijing market at that time and ended up only being sold in hotels and certain restaurants.

The success of one marketing approach and the relative failure of the other demonstrates that foreign companies wishing to sell products in China need to aware of two important factors. The first is that presentation is just as important as issues of price and quality. The second is that Chinese consumers' social psychology must be researched and taken into account.

Chinese consumers strictly choose the colour of the packaging to serve different social occasions. It has been said that Chinese people traditionally like the colour red in packaging. Nowadays, this is only partially true. Chinese consumers choose goods with red packaging when they want to give a wedding gift, or a present to the aged, or for their own consumption at some traditional Chinese festival. For Chinese people, the colour red looks joyful and represents prosperity and good luck. They may, however, select different-coloured packaging at other times. For example, many young women in China prefer 'magnificent colours' for the packaging of clothes or cosmetics. Only the colour dark blue must still be used with caution in packaging, because consumers, especially old people, sometimes identify it with death.

Changing tastes in colour preferences can be seen in China's modern-day wedding ceremony. In the 'old days', a Chinese bride would wear only red on her wedding day. Nowadays, most brides wear various sets of clothes in different colours, especially in urban areas where consumer demand and awareness are high. A modern Chinese bride may wear several sets of new clothes at different times during the ceremony. A bride's change of clothes includes a traditional red wedding dress, Western-style wedding clothes in pure white and an array of fashionable clothes in various colours. Chinese perceptions of colours are summarised in Table 8.2. The same colour may sometimes have both a 'good' and a 'bad' symbolic significance, depending on the occasion or context.

Table 8.2 Chinese Perceptions of Colours

Colour	Perception	Colour	Perception
Grey	Conservative, Gentle, Inexpensive	Maroon	Noble, High Quality, Expensive
Blue	Bad Luck, Death, Ordinary quality	Brown	Staid, Reliable, Inexpensive
Light Blue	Young, High Quality, Peaceful	Black	Powerful, Staid, Reliable, or alternatively, Evil
Red	Fortune, Happiness, Love, Propitious, Joyfulness	White	Pure, Peaceful, Delicate or, Bad Luck, Death (especially in rural areas)
Yellow	Progressive, Active, Propitious	Green	Youthfulness, Active Vigour

As a final note, the Chinese Commercial Department stipulates that all product labels must contain a detailed description of the product, including the address of the producer and the place of manufacture. Labels on imported products must be in legible Chinese characters.

Advertising

The influence of advertising in China is extremely powerful. This is due to Chinese consumer psychology and the high profile that most forms of media enjoy among Chinese audiences. Since the government administrates China's media, especially television, radio and important newspapers, ordinary Chinese trust most reports about commerce or trade as long as these stories are presented as 'official news'. Information in the form of television advertisements plays a powerful role in terms of social or consumer reference groups.

Case Study: Using 'Golden Time'

An alcoholic drink named Kong-fu JiaJiu (which in Chinese means 'a spirit especially made in the Confucian Mansion') was one of many almost unknown brands of liqueur on the Chinese market in the early 1990s. At the time older and well-established brands like Maotai, Wulyang Ye, and Luzhou Daqu totally dominated the market. The producer of the new liqueur wisely decided to promote his product through an intensive advertising campaign. The producer borrowed a large amount of money to finance advertising on the best television channel in China — China Central Television (CCTV) — during 'golden time'. The advertising fee for this campaign was about 100 million RMB yuan (about US$12 million), but it resulted in amazing commercial success and since then, Kong-fu JiaJiu has been continually advertised on CCTV, with an annual advertising budget of about 100 million RMB yuan.

Media Selection

For many MNCs, the intensive use of advertising to promote brands is seen as a key approach to the Chinese market. However, the choice of where to advertise in China requires careful thought because of the complicated administrative organisation of the media in China. It is easy for foreign companies to waste resources by choosing to advertise at the wrong level or using regional media.

There are no purely private media in China. In principle the media are all supervised by the government at different levels. The official media has a powerful impact on the Chinese people. Due to the political system in China, the government controls the media nation-wide, though to a lesser extent in the regional areas. In particular, national media are tightly controlled and supervised by the Propaganda Department of the CCP, the Ministry of Radio, Film and Television of the State Council, and the State News Publishing Bureau. Since the government finances the Chinese media, they are all ranked as government organisations. A wide variety of consumer demands and the complicated Chinese political system makes the selection of advertising in China a tough task in terms of regions and marketing targets.

China's media are normally divided into four categories based on the hierarchical administration of government. It is important to know the differences in role, coverage and authority of these media for the effective promotion of product.

1. *Media administrated by the Central Government*

   Many media organisations like the China Central Television Station (CCTV), the China Central Radio Station (CCRS), the China News Agency, the Xinyuan News Agency, *The People's Daily* and *The Qiushi Magazine* are directly administered by the central government. These media enjoy massive audiences — viewers, listeners and readers — who collectively have a powerful influence on Chinese business practices. For instance, almost 300 million people watch CCTV every day. *The People's Daily*, which is run by the CCP, has an equally extensive distribution, as every local branch of the CCP across China subscribes.

Moreover, many of the central government ministries operate their own newspapers, focusing on their own particular professional fields. At present, these include: *The Guangming Daily* (run by the state Education Commission); *The Economic Daily* (run by the State Economic and Trade Commission); *The Legal Daily* (run by the Ministry of Justice); *The Science and Technology* Daily (run by the State Science and Technology Commission); *The China Business Times* (run by the China Federation of Industry and Business); and *The Sport Daily* (run by the State Physical Culture and Sports Commission). These newspapers not only cater for professional groups, but are also distributed across China for general readership.

In China all of these media are allowed to display commercials. Advertising fees for CCTV are usually higher than other forms of Chinese media because CCTV broadcasts nationwide, even worldwide, and enjoys a very high profile among the Chinese people. Television is usually the first option for promotion for companies that possess a China-wide distribution network and have deep pockets. The effectiveness of promotion in this media category in China is pre-eminent.

2. *Media Administrated by Provincial and Municipal Governments*

In China, provincial governments and city administrations with provincial status administer some media organisations directly.

Every province and municipality under the direct control of the central government has their own television station, radio station and at least one newspaper. The influence of these media mostly covers provincial or individual city areas. However, with the development of a satellite system in China, some of these television and radio stations can now broadcast their programs to other provinces. For instance, Beijing receives programs broadcast by television stations in Shanghai, the Tibet Autonomous Region, Yuennian Province and so on.

The media at this level are the most powerful in terms of advertising influence for targeted regions and they play a crucial role in promoting commercial success. The media in these areas are tightly controlled by local government for both political and business reasons. Parochialism is a serious problem. Apart from local government policies, regions play a unique role in promoting local products. This involves the practical exclusion of competitors' products from other regions. Some local governments at this level even stipulate that only local newspapers and a few central government newspapers can be sold in the region and its cities.

3. *Media Administered by Municipal or County Governments*

Every municipal and county government in China operates a television station, radio network, and one or more newspapers. These media are the primary means by which local residents obtain news and information, including details of local job recruitment. Movies, documentaries and drama series occupy most of the broadcasting time of these regional TV stations.

These local media are an effective means of promoting products, but only on a regional basis. Advertising rates are lower than in metropolitan areas. These media are less controlled by central government, so their news reports or regular columns are a little more flexible. Most newspapers and television stations in this category are very popular among local consumers. For example, *The China Business Times, The Beijing Evening* (in Beijing City), *The Yangcheng Evening* (in Guangzhou City), the *Xinmin Evening*, (in Shanghai City), Beijing Television, Orient Television (Shanghai City) and Guangdou Television, are very popular both locally and provincially. Advertising fees are lower than for centrally controlled media, as their broadcast or distribution coverage area is smaller, being more focused on specific audiences or readership groups. They are suitable for advertisements promoting products in certain specified geographical or professional fields of interest.

4. *Media Administrated by Large State-Owned Enterprises*

In China, many state-owned enterprises employ as many as 100,000 people. Being like a small society, SOEs not only have their own hospital, school, shops, sports facilities and child care centres, but also have their own television station, radio network, and newspaper or newspapers. The main purpose of these internal media is to provide employees and their families with information about their particular enterprise's activities and organisational work performance. These outlets also sell advertising space, although the quality of advertising is not as high as in other categories. However, enterprise-based television, radio and newspapers can be a useful means of promotion if you want to explore the market of a particular target community. The advantages are that they are popular with local residents; the rate of watching, listening or reading is high; and the advertising tariffs are low.

In summary, although all the various forms and categories of Chinese media described above are financed by the government and no purely commercially-run media exist, they are all allowed to engage in commercial advertising. Indeed, commercial advertising has been one of the main sources of revenue for many government enterprises in the media industry, because the government's financial allocation is insufficient to allow them to run their operations effectively. Communication enterprises such as CCTV depend on advertising income to maintain their operations. They also depend on advertising revenue to provide employees with various forms of basic welfare.

Internet Users

At the beginning of 2001 there were over 22.5 million Internet users in China. A survey by The China Internet Network Information Centre reported that 3.64 million Chinese citizens leased line connections, with dial-up users numbering 15.43 million.

The survey reported that 23.4 per cent of Chinese web sites were hosted in Beijing, 14.24 per cent in Gunagdong province, and 10.61 per cent in Shanghai. The majority of the participants surveyed were males between the ages of 18 and 24 with a bachelor's degree. Slightly more than 60 per cent of the partici-pants accessed the Internet from home. Slightly less than 44 per cent accessed the Web from a work place. The top service was email, with the users surveyed logging on to the Internet an average of 13.66 hours per week. China is presently at what is called 'the applications stage' of IT development and will move to the 'services stage' soon.

Advertising Strategies

As outlined, China has a number of very different market segmentations and is typified by unique subsets of consumer psychology. A number of strategies have proved effective for advertising.

1. *Halo effect of Celebrities*

    Because the Chinese market is immature, there is no solid implementation of regulations or laws, on misleading advertisements, false products and brands. Consumers need to make sure that the products they are going to buy are reliable as a particular advertisement indicates. They believe that celebrities will endorse accurate information, as celebrities are assumed to value their reputation. At the same time, the association of a celebrity with a particular brand name enhances the status of those who go out and buy the same product. The upper classes like to demonstrate their status by using a particularly prestigious brand name, while the lower classes similarly seek to advance their status by the same means. In other words, product prestige is leveraged by celebrity promotion. Using a celebrity to promote a brand is not a new idea but in China it has proved to be extremely effective.

2. *Fashion and Value*

    Chinese consumers are likely to consider whether a particular purchase is worthwhile by comparing price, function and brand popularity. As demonstrated above, Chinese people do not easily give up their traditional value of thrift and the true value of a product must at least be worth the price that they pay for it. Value for money and fashion are their driving motives, but shopping can also be a social activity amongst some Chinese consumers and on many occasions they like share the enjoyment of large purchase with friends and relatives and to show off the proof of their prudent purchase decision. An advertisement which indicates that a product is well worth its price and at the same time fashionable, is attractive to many Chinese consumers.

3. *'Soft' Advertisements*

A company producing a brand of mineral water receptacle was nearly bankrupt in 1991 because it could not sell its product in the Chinese market. A soft advertising campaign saved this enterprise. As the sponsor of a television comedy series, the firm's product was deliberately used in the series by the filmmaker. The comedy was very popular across China, as was the product whose sales increased dramatically.

Hard advertising, like most commercial advertising in the West, is designed to promote a particular product or enterprise image. A second type of advertisement, described in Western marketing theory as 'publicity', conveys favourable information about a company, goods or services, and appears in the mass media as a news item. Chinese people refer to this type of advertisement as 'soft' advertising. For soft advertising, the public relations managers of Chinese enterprises may provide journalists with a certain kind of benefit or convenience in appreciation for their co-operation. In return the journalists will be expected to guarantee to report information in the form of a news story. In the reported story, information about the enterprise, including management, technology and production capacity, are described in detail, as well as the qualities and advantages of the particular enterprise's goods or services.

Compared with hard advertising, the latter has some distinct advantages. Most importantly, soft advertising wins the trust of most Chinese consumers who are not always inclined to put their faith in commercial advertisements. Their general distrust of commerce is based on their experience of China's immature market, where illegal activities are still rampant and where the traditional perception of business as crafty and unscrupulous still has currency. Audiences and readers feel that a news report published in the media is based on facts and contains less commercial overstatement about products. Moreover, soft advertising not only promotes goods and services, but also can also effectively raise the image of a particular enterprise. Due to the competitiveness of the current Chinese market, the image of an enterprise is growing in importance and increasingly a concern in management circles. The cost of providing benefits to journalists for soft advertising is much less than the cost of hard advertising.

Approximately a thousand TV series or documentaries are produced in China annually. Only a few are sponsored by the government. The production of most of these television series and documentaries relies on sponsorship. Chinese enterprises and companies are the main sources of this funding. These programs are seen as an effective way of promoting the profile of organisations and their products. Program sponsorship is also categorised as soft advertising by the Chinese commercial community.

Organising Advertising

With the increase in the number of media outlets, China's advertising industry has developed in leaps and bounds. Advertising has already become the main means of promotion for most enterprises. Before the Open Door reforms there were fifty television stations in China.

By 1995 however, there were 3125, an increase of sixty times from 1977. The current number is ten times as many as the number of television stations in the United States; twenty-five times as many as the number in Japan; and 260 times as many as the number of British stations. The growth rate of television stations across China and the government's positive encouragement of advertising have facilitated the development of the world's most dynamic advertising industry. In preparation for the competition of foreign media with the entry of China into WTO, many television stations, and newspapers are currently being merged to form larger media corporations.

The first commercial advertisement on Chinese television was broadcast at 6:59 p.m. — i.e. prime time, just before the evening news program on CCTV — on 15th March 1979. Since then, the advertising industry in China has been growing at the rate of 40 per cent, which is 30 per cent higher than the average growth rate of China's economy overall. The turnover of China's advertising industry was respectively 20 billion RMB yuan (about US$2.413 billion) in 1994; 30 billion RMB yuan (about US$3.628 billion) in 1995; and up to 38 billion RMB yuan (about US$ 4.59 billion) in 1996.

China's first Advertising Act became effective on 1st July 1995. The advertising industry in China has since enjoyed constant official support through the reform of commercial law relating to advertising and promotion. For example, CCTV first implemented a policy that the advertising fee for 'golden time' (from 7:30 p.m. to 7:35 p.m. right after the evening news) should be auctioned to the highest bidder. This means that the advertising fee for 'golden time' on CCTV has no fixed price. An advertiser who pays the highest price will get his or her advertisement displayed on CCTV at this time.

Some foreign advertising experts have claimed that the growth of China's advertising industry is like a "reinless horse" and estimate that China will become the largest advertising market in the world by the year 2010.

In China, all types of media have an advertising department, which specifies advertising rates and deals with clients. The rates of advertising vary considerably between regions, media forms, popularity, and scope of coverage. Another way to place advertisements in the media is to employ an advertising agency. The advertising agency is responsible for negotiating with the media to arrange all advertising details — broadcasting time, column space, etc. Most Chinese advertising agencies charge clients a fee for arranging advertising, including their design and production. They also charge the particular media organisation a certain percentage of the advertising costs as a commission or as an agency fee. Advertising charges are based on market prices. However, sometimes a client may get a better deal with a particular media outlet because of a pre-existing, long-term business relationship. In the light of China's Advertising Act, any enterprise wishing to advertise its product or service must show its business licence and product qualifications to both the advertising agency and the media organisation.

Soft advertising in China is not free and has to be paid for in other ways, especially if the commercial purpose of this type of advertisement is met. In developed countries, although an organisation does not necessarily have to pay for mass-media exposure, preparing press releases and persuading media personalities to print or broadcast their 'news items' does take resources and costs money. The same is even truer in China. Publicity, or more correctly, soft advertising may be very costly, especially if a Chinese enterprise a particular media has been selected for their soft advertising campaign. Time or space resources in the media in China, particularly in popular newspapers and on television channels, remain in extremely short supply. Furthermore newspapers with a nation-wide distribution cannot offer one single additional page for publication without China's State Administration of News, Press and Publication department granting permission for them to do so. For this reason Chinese journalists and editors are in a very powerful position to decide what news and which stories should be reported. They can easily refuse to report information about an enterprise that is keen for publicity. This is one of the reasons why it is important to have a good relationship with the various departments of the media and with journalists.

Benefits for journalists and editors could mean money, the use of goods and services, or payment in kind — banquets, travel, holidays, etc. Actually a journalist who obtains benefit for reporting a particular story is violating official regulations, but their low income puts them in a position where they are quickly tempted. Some journalists' incomes from unofficial sources may be higher than from their formal salaries.

Public Relations
Public relations has been extremely popular in China since 1987. When the idea was first introduced into China most businesspeople and managers misunderstood the concept. They regarded public relations as a procedure where personal relationship networks were established in order to facilitate the attainment of corporate goals.

In the late 1980s, demand outstripped supply in the Chinese market, especially in respect to raw materials and financial resources. These resources were tightly controlled by a small number of powerful individuals within specific governmental departments. This led businesspeople and managers to concentrate on a three-way relationship between their enterprise, officialdom and their suppliers, instead of their relationship with their customers, suppliers, employees and other participants in the market place. In China's centrally planned economy, it was the manufacturers who decided what consumers wanted and only produced what they believed was needed.

With the development of the Chinese economy since the 1990s, a sellers' market has turned into a buyers' market. Chinese managers and businesspeople have been forced to accept market competition and have had to agree that consumer demand should now drive production. A company's competitive capacity now decides the fate of most enterprises. The focus is now consumer-oriented, at least in the minds of many managers (although personal relationships with officials and other businesspeople are still recognised as crucial to success in business). Consequently, since the mid-1990s, public relations have come to be correctly interpreted by Chinese managers and businesspeople. This in turn helps the company towards accomplishing key marketing goals and management strategies.

Many Chinese businesses, including state-owned, collective-owned, or private enterprises, have set up public relations departments. The main task of these departments is to communicate with the public; to resolve conflicts between the enterprise and customers; to report information about public demand to top management; and to assist management in deciding on correct marketing strategies. These departments are now referred to as 'the creators of the enterprise image'. At present, there are four types of public relations activities operating in China.

1. *Publicity-Orientated PR*

   This focuses on promoting the image of a particular enterprise in the public forum. Qualified Chinese public relations managers often have good connections with the media having worked as either journalists or editors before taking up their position. They are responsible for maintaining a good working relationship with their former colleagues. They make use of these relationships to report enterprise information in the form of soft advertising in order to highlight the profile of the enterprise.

2. *Socially-Oriented PR*

   This focuses on establishing extensive business networks with key social players. As emphasised in previous chapters, informal relationships are often more effective than formal ones in helping to find solutions to particular management problems. This not only makes the job of a public relations manager in China very complicated but also very subtle. A good public relations manager must be able to communicate well and get on well with others. He or she must also be able to organise a wide variety of public and private activities, such as business openings, anniversary celebrations, and the launching of a new product on the market. To raise a particular company's corporate profile, a good public relations manager must be able to ensure the involvement of a broad range of VIP guests, government officials and wealthy customers. Suppliers, other businesspeople, local and regional officials, bankers, representatives of the Price Bureau, the Tax Office, and the Department of Administration of Industry and Commence, must all be invited to an appropriate reception, dinner or opening. They must also be included in any recreational activity that is organised by the public relations manager for the benefit of foreign counterparts. Each and every relevant person must be contacted in an appropriate way, and at a minimum of cost to the enterprise.

3. *Consultative-Oriented PR*

This focuses on the analysis of information and data. It provides management with feedback about the enterprise's products and image. In China consultative public relations usually includes activities such as customer-focused professional sales and marketing seminars and the evaluation of survey results or complaints.

4. *Public-Good-Oriented PR*

This is designed to raise the profile of an enterprise through the sponsorship of public welfare activities. For both individual businesspeople and their respective organisations, a good reputation is paramount. Businesspeople or enterprises take part in philanthropic activities for reasons other than simply effectively promoting their product. Chinese business culture emphasises the value of 'face' and businesspeople and enterprises will feel a sense of shame if they are seen as being stingy. A show of public generosity 'wins face'. In addition, some businesspeople in China are still worried about the traditional view of commerce as something basically immoral. Businesspeople will try to ameliorate a negative impression of their company by engaging in charitable activities.

Many non-profit, or non-business organisations will take advantage of a particular situation to seek sponsorship for a large project by organising social activities that are intended to have a strong and positive influence on public opinion. A medium or large enterprise may receive a great number of sponsorship invitations every day. These non-profit organisations may be governmental or non-governmental, or they may be schools or universities. A local government authority may ask a firm to sponsor a bridge or some other construction project. The reward for this support is often naming rights. Not surprisingly, sporting organisations in China are almost all sponsored by business.

In China, there are always too many invitations for enterprises to donate money in order to establish good corporate citizenship credentials. Enterprises have difficulty donating money to them all, and so risk causing disappointment, thereby losing 'face' For very practical reasons, China's State Council has stipulated that an enterprise has the right to reject any sponsorship demand. However, sometimes enterprises are forced to take part in public welfare activities, though they may not have their hearts in it. They must however, often agree to support certain charitable projects because of concerns about 'face' protection and long-term personal relationships. Hence, there is a common saying in Chinese public relations that 'the best public relations expert is not the one who can satisfy all sponsorship demands, but the one who can maintain a good relationship with others even after rejecting their demand for sponsorship'.

China's rapidly changing market and complicated political and social systems have meant that qualified public relations managers are very much in demand. An expert public relations manager must understand the characteristics of the Chinese market; be able to establish friendly relationships with various governmental departments and the media; and possess experience, professional knowledge and skills in a wide range of interpersonal activities. As previously mentioned, in China it is easy to find skilled workers, but it is very difficult to recruit qualified managers, including public relations managers. An enterprise would consider itself extremely fortunate if it could attract a senior or experienced public relations manager. The higher the managerial position a person holds, the more public relations knowledge, experience or interpersonal skills he or she must possess.

Distribution
Current Obstacles

The allocation of all goods was completely controlled by the central government according to a central plan before the late 1970s. Since the Open Door policy, China's distribution channels have improved dramatically, with distribution being decentralised and divided up among thousands of new, independent dealers. Today, most industrial products and commodities, with the exception of some important agricultural products, are distributed according to market demand and priced by the dealers themselves. Meanwhile, infrastructure facilities for the delivery of goods have been greatly improved, particularly in the eastern part of China. Despite these very positive developments, distribution in China, does not compare very favourably with other more developed countries. The main problem is that cross-country distribution networks remain undeveloped, with regional blockades effectively hampering the free flow of certain goods into some territories.

Protectionism in the Provinces

China has always had a traditional distribution system — a loose network of local dealers scattered throughout the country. This network was very inefficient and is even worse now because of increasing regional trade blockades. China is not one market but many, based on provinces and even cities. Parochialism is a common feature of life from the provincial level to the third rank of city level. It makes it extremely difficult for both domestic and foreign companies to distribute products through channels across China and to gain a national presence. Often local governments adopt policies that increase the difficulties for imports into their territory, while limiting the exportation of useful raw materials from their territory. Sometimes they ban the import of foreign goods and services altogether in order to protect local products and services, even though these local products or services may be of lower quality and less competitive in price.

One protectionist strategy that is frequently used is to set up different taxation policies for local and non-local brands. Non-local brands distributed in their territory are charged more tax and other business-related fees than local brands. For instance, the Shanghai government stipulates that governmental organisations and state-owned enterprises should buy cars made by manufactories under the governance of the Shanghai municipality. Under this system, the Santana model produced by a joint venture of Volkswagen and Shanghai Automotive Industrial Corp. has become the government-mandated choice for Shanghai's taxi fleet. At the same time, the Shanghai government charges both a higher registration fee and sales taxes on cars manufactured in other provinces. This is two to three times as much as for cars produced locally. Customers buying cars made outside Shanghai have to pay about 10 per cent on top of the final purchase price. This effectively prevents most Shanghainese from buying private cars from outside producers.

A beer producer based in Shandong Province, was located only 150 kilometres away from another city with a population of 8 million people in Jiang-su Province. This brewer wanted to sell its brand in the neighbouring city. Unfortunately the municipal government of the other city banned the sale of imported beers. To break through these sorts of internal trade blockades within China, both Chinese and foreign businesspeople have to deal with local distributors and officials in each and every area, region or city that they wish to sell their products. This is both complicated and confusing and increases business costs enormously.

Due to an uneven development of the economy in different areas, many local officials and manufacturers wish to protect their own regional trade interests. They claim that they must safeguard local products and industries to guarantee local government income tax revenue and employment levels. Another excuse is that different provinces each have their own administrative affiliations with industries within their respective areas of jurisdiction and should not become involved with businesses interests outside their region. Actually, the reason for local governments doing adopting this stance is not simply because of their concern for the local economy, but also because of a deeper, political reason. Firstly, local officials need to use the growth of the local economy to prove their performance to their superiors. Secondly, they wish to further their own personal interests by manipulating local trade. Many regional officials often abuse their autonomy in the pursuit of personal gain — in implementing a policy of local protectionism, they can easily tap into a 'black' income based on local and non-local businesspeople seeking to gain their favour in order to operate a business under their particular local 'regime'.

Local protectionism is also a reason for the violation of intellectual property rights. In order to establish more effective nation-wide marketing networks and maintain national revenue, the Chinese central government has used administrative means to limit the negative influence of regional trade protectionism. At the same time the government has encouraged the development of 'chain trade'. It seems that the effectiveness of these policies is limited at present. A few of China's largest companies have established a national distribution chain, although they still don't have access to all major Chinese territories.

Conflict between Retailers and Wholesalers

Vertical distribution conflict easily occurs between manufacturers and retailers in China. Currently, the Chinese market is very competitive with both costs and sales increasing. In the main cities of Beijing, Shanghai and Guangzhou, retailers generally charge about 30-40 per cent, of the actual sales price. There is an unwritten rule in the Beijing market that retailers usually do not pay a trade invoice until three months after the goods have been sold. Retailers sometimes further delay payment or the return of unsold stock because of difficulties with their turnover. Conflicts of this nature can cause the breakdown of established distribution channels.

Marketing Channels

Establishing effective marketing channels is a one of the greatest challenges for both Chinese and foreign marketers. Here are some key points in the design of a marketing channel.

Firstly, a channel network must concentrate on building up bases in three to five large cities where commerce is already highly developed. The network can then be expanded to other cities after initial successes in the market place. This tactic is regarded as 'go ahead steadily and strike sure blows'. While building up bases of distribution, a company can obtain sales experience and learn how to operate a marketing channel network in China. It gives a foreign marketer an opportunity to sound out the opinion of Chinese consumers, which in turn would provide important information about future growth rates and an expansion distribution networks.

Areas covered by expanded distribution must be carefully assessed in order to reduce delivery costs, since China's current transport infrastructure is still inadequate and transportation costs could be very high for long-distance deliveries. Selecting areas for market expansion that are near to the initial distribution point(s) is strongly advised.

Secondly, it is vital to develop a good relationship with both local dealers who have financial strength, networks and officials who have political influence. The Chinese market is large and its distribution is difficult to manage. A producer needs to make use of local dealers' relationships — *guanxi* — to develop a market share is an effective way. Xerox of Shanghai, for instance, has used this means to dramatically increase its sales across China. It credits much of its 43 per cent market share in China to the friendships that were developed over time by local dealers. An agent or company with a high profile, wide *guanxi* network and strong financial strength is better able to help a Chinese or foreign manufacturer develop their market speedily. Sellers must also establish a good relationship with officials at every level in the administrative hierarchy in order to break trade blockades and establish unimpeded distribution throughout China. They will need to apply the appropriate approaches introduced in Chapter Six.

Thirdly, there are a number of special sales strategies which can be adopted to enhance distribution. Speciality stores are one of the best sales pathways. Department stores and plazas aside, speciality stores appeal very much to Chinese consumers and some well-known foreign fashion designers and producers have succeeded in China by selling their products through such retail outlets. Children's clothing, and men's and women's fashion wear, as well as other luxury merchandise, can sometimes be sold more effectively in a speciality stores than in other types of retail outlet because Chinese consumers, especially the young and the wealthy, prefer to purchase well-known or 'trend' brands. A speciality store will easily establish a particular brand among Chinese consumers who are otherwise swamped with competing merchandise. Supply conferences and exhibitions are also a good way of establishing successful and lasting distribution networks in China.

Local knowledge of business in China's urban areas is very important. China's major cities all tend to differ from one another in terms of their industries, the nature of businesses and subcultures. Some foreign companies prefer Hong Kong as a base to enter the Chinese market because they believe it has the advantages of English language proficiency and the knowledge of modern business practices. To a certain extent, this is true, but it is advisable to choose agents in Hong Kong cautiously. Some Hong Kong based agents are qualified and enjoy reasonable business relationships with Mainland China, but there are others who are not qualified or experienced in doing business or else charge enormous fees for providing middleman services. To opt for Hong Kong as a way to enter the Chinese market place can entail a number of potential risks or hidden costs. Often the agents themselves do not really understand the complexities of business in Mainland China and are not a part of any business network there. Lacking any local business knowledge of China, these agents will typically use the fees they charge foreign companies to buy information or *guanxi*. Ultimately, the cost and risk of using Hong Kong-based middlemen may sometimes be much higher than employing a direct approach to Mainland China, where many people can now speak fluent English and possess extensive in-country networks.

Some foreign companies have a mistaken perception of Chinese cities and draw analogies between, for example, Beijing and Washington, or Canberra, as the political and administrative capital of the nation, rather than as a business centre *per se*. They believe that only Shanghai, which is frequently compared to New York or Sydney, is the best place for doing business. Beijing actually is a key business and network centre as well and many successful MNCs have realised this and have located their business operations in Beijing, with branch offices in other cities, such as Shanghai, Shangzhen and Guangzhou.

Case Study: Unilever's Fast Network Development

Unilever began the challenge of building up their distributive network with a few core cities in the summer of 1994. They then rapidly developed their network across China. This strategy began with Unilever placing their ice cream products in selected markets. Apart from advertising, Unilever very effectively promoted their product by offering hundreds of dealers and sales people electronic vending vehicles free of charge. These were attractively decorated and featured strong brand symbols. By 1995, from this small core market, the company developed distribution and sales networks in 129 large cities. Unilever applied the lessons they had learned in the core market group to a wide range of new and different product categories. The company then implemented their second and third rank of sales agency strategy in medium cities and affiliated counties. Unilever also restructured their major sales divisions to ensure the quality of sales staff. This included providing sales agents with proper training. Unilever quickly channelled their distributive network across 500 cities, 1500 out of a total of 1800 regional counties and one third of the 47000 towns in China. A national distributive network was firmly and rapidly established. The combined effect of a mature network, well trained staff, and effective advertising lead to Unilever nearly doubling their annual China sales volume from 2.3 billion to 4.0 billion RMB Yuan since 1998.

Despite the accelerated pace of their distribution expansion, Unilever followed the following principles:

- They built up bases in large cities first where commerce was already highly developed and equipped with successful and experiences sales staff.
- They then gradually and steadily pushed out the boundaries of their existing distribution networks, utilising their expanding knowledge of the Chinese market, to include a broader range of sales territories.
- Unilever then quickly and smoothly developed their distributing network cross the breath of continental China.
- The Unilever experience clearly demonstrates that a staged, careful, and appropriate strategy, which takes account of local opportunities and conditions can yield amazing success.

Chapter 9

How to Thrive in Business

According to a 1997 World Bank report, China is at an "economic crossroads". One turn in the road could lead to unprecedented commercial success. This, the World Bank states, is dependent on the Chinese Government's continued program of reform, especially in respect to good administration and sound economic policy. On the other hand, a wrong turn could result in a catastrophe — i.e. if the fundamentals of Deng Xiao Ping's Open Door policy are rejected and China again closes its doors to the international community. The same report lists China's strengths as its high savings rate, pragmatic economic reforms, relative stability, disciplined and literate labour force, supportive diaspora and growing administrative capacity. These strengths combined with a massive market and highly competitive wage rates, together with WTO entry and the 2008 Olympic Games, makes China a very attractive place to do business. Currently there are many foreign companies enjoying steady profitable growth in the Chinese market. This has been largely due to these same companies' extensive knowledge of China's unique business culture as well as their own local experience in marketing and sales. This chapter concludes all of the topics covered in this book by a discussion of the six 'P's of successful business in China: 'Patience', 'Power' in finance, 'Predisposition' in policies and relationships, 'Personnel', 'Protection' with legal security and the 'Perspective' of cultural sensitivity.

F oreign businesspeople should fully prepare themselves before attempting to enter the Chinese market. This preparation should include an evaluation of strategic risks. In China, as elsewhere, the business rule of thumb is that the higher the risk, the greater the possible return. The following advice will be invaluable for foreign businesspeople who want to weigh up the risks and benefits of participating in the world's largest market. They can be summarised as the "six Ps": patience, power, predisposition, personnel, protection and perspective.

The Six 'P's

1. Patience: *Psychological Preparation*

If foreign businesspeople wish to successfully invest capital, establish a joint venture or sell products in the Chinese market, they must be patient. It takes time to succeed in the Chinese business environment and if foreign businesspeople expect to gain an immediate return on their capital or infrastructure investment in China they will be disappointed.

The Chinese market is huge but immature. It takes a long time for foreigners to establish a strong business base. Setting up a business takes time. The negotiation processes described in Chapter Four are complex. In most large enterprises, negotiation procedures usually occur in two phases. The first phase involves making contact with interested parties, information collection, and the evaluation of desirable partners. In the second phase, front-line negotiators submit their reports for assessment by the company's executive hierarchy. This often involves several rounds before a final decision is reached. Registering a business can also take a long time, though it is much faster nowadays. Currently it takes up to three months to obtain the registration approval. Secondly, one has to wait for a degree of mutual trust to be established between prospective partners. Trust is a basic condition for conducting effective business in China, facilitating negotiations, establishing substantial business co-operation, and smoothly solving disputes. Chinese businesspeople take this trust-building process as an essential part of business. Foreign businesspeople ignore this feature of the Chinese market at their peril. As in any international strategic alliance, where trust and commitment are necessary components in the relationship (Parkhe, 1998), Chinese businesspeople will not get involved in substantial transactions with international counterparts until solid trust is built.

Thirdly, it takes time to establish a *guanxi* network, yet this continues to be a crucial component in any successful business venture in China today. For example, a Chinese equipment buyer may prefer to pay a higher price for a low quality or sub-standard technical product simply because the supplier is one of his *guanxi* connections. Gaining access to commercial networks and then utilising them to further one's own interests are a necessary, yet very time-consuming aspect, of doing business.

There are also a number of structural problems inherent in China's transitional economy. Trade protectionism and corruption still exists; the administrative system of official regulations is under-developed; changes in Chinese commercial law have not yet been fully implemented; and some Chinese businesspeople simply will not conduct business openly.

Although some types of immoral or anti-competitive behaviour will be corrected, or at least contained, with China joining the WTO, a mature and transparent market will not appear overnight. At present, Chinese managers have to adapt themselves to these to these negative factors, including bribery and corrupt business practices. Judging from a survey carried out by Shanghai's *Wenhiu Daily* in 1997, which examined Chinese manager's tolerance of immoral conduct in commerce, overcoming corruption in China will be a long process.

Table 9.1 Chinese Managers' Tolerance of Immoral Behaviour

Types of immoral behaviour	Degree of tolerance
Bribery of persons in charge	79.8%
Bribing customers	71.3%
Under weighting goods for sale	55.45%
Dishonest advertising	55.0%
Evading taxation	18.35%
Environmental pollution	3.3%

Source: *Wenhiu Daily*, 14 March 1997

As already detailed in previous chapters, since 1978 the Chinese government has adopted an Open Door policy towards foreign investment in China and is making great progress towards changing its centrally planned economy. Nevertheless, the government still controls the marketplace and its policies can place obstacles in front of domestic or foreign businesses just as easily as granting concessions. Moreover, these polices are sometimes changed at short notice, with negative consequences for a particular sector of the business community. An example of this is the Chinese government's favoured policy towards foreign investment in the Chinese beer industry.

Case Study: 'New' Protectionism?

Foreign beers / beverages were basically a prohibited import into China before the 1978 economic reforms. The growth rate of beer consumption in the PRC has been running at about 20 per cent annually since the late 1980s. It is estimated that China will become the world's largest beer market in the near future. Many foreign beer producers established themselves in China as joint, or wholly-owned ventures. A trade war ensued between competing foreign interests, on the one hand, and foreign and domestic beer producers on the other. In this trade war, domestic Chinese beer producers suffered substantial losses. Soon afterwards, the Chinese government decided to make a number of 'policy adjustments' in order to protect China's domestic beer industry and from 1996 limits were re-imposed on the operations of foreign beer producers in the Chinese market. This modified policy caused substantial short-term losses for foreign investors. Because international beer companies had planned ahead and invested substantial sums of money in promotion, advertising, distribution and increased production capacity, their loss was especially great. This new protectionism may only be a temporary deviation from a longer-term policy, but according to some foreign beer producers the damage has already been done.

A very strong signal was sent to the international business community that the Chinese government was prepared, if necessary, to move the goal posts when it suited them. Clearly a long-term perspective and a great deal of patience are prerequisites for doing business in China, though some degree of uncertainty will disappear now that China has joined the WTO.

The emergence of the Chinese domestic market is difficult to anticipate with the continuous reform in every area of industry. Values and incomes are changing as are individual purchasing power and buyer behaviour. Equally, the Chinese market is bitterly competitive. As the domestic market opens up to foreign competition, an enormous variety of consumers have become available. Each has their own domestic and imported competitors. All products compete for quality, presentation and price. Quite often a number of MNCs are competing with each other for the exposure of similar products in the Chinese market, as are, many local Chinese manufacturers. All are very conscious of how acute market competition will be, now that China has entered WTO as well as how to play the globalisation game effectively. Many Chinese firms have learnt a great deal about internal management and marketing since 1978. They know how to exploit the advantages of local networks, cultural knowledge and competitive practices. Their business strategies are improving and their business competence is increasing, which means that they can often compete with foreign producers both in terms of price and quality. For example, Chinese-made TVs are winning market share from well-known Japanese brands, which have virtually monopolised the Chinese market for the last fifteen years.

Chinese consumers have many options to consider before making a purchase. They have developed sophisticated tastes and tend to compare goods as much as possible in terms of their price, status indication, popularity, function and so on before purchasing an expensive item. This makes it difficult to introduce a new product into the Chinese market and even more difficult to ensure its popularity. In this huge, changing and immature market, it takes time for the consumer to first recognise and then select a new product. In this respect, identifying the right strategic steps and employing the best promotion are necessary for success. Huge profits will flow once a brand becomes popular — P&G, IBM and Coca-Cola, are good examples of a successful mix of policy and practice in China today (Xue, 2000). Taken together, gaining and maintaining growth in the Chinese market requires foreign investors to be patient. Foreign investors need to be sufficiently prepared in terms of long-term business strategies.

2. Power: *Financial Strength*

Running a successful business in China requires strong financial power. The market is like an ocean and a business with weak financial power is like a small boat that can easily capsize in economic bad weather while a business with great financial strength is like an ocean-going super tanker that can survive even the roughest conditions. Practice and analysis has shown that entering the Chinese market requires very deep pockets. Initially profits are elusive until he foreign company learns to adapt to the subtleties of Chinese business culture and the realities of the Chinese market. This includes determining how much capital is required to promote goods or services. Some business expenses in China can be higher than in many Western countries. For example, advertising fees and office rental in Shanghai and Beijing are amongst the highest in the world. Advertising rates in China have a direct relationship to business opportunities and the promotional effectiveness of the official media — television, radio and newspapers — that is unmatched anywhere else in the world. The official media in China, for instance, have millions and sometimes over 1 billion loyal listeners, viewers or readers. Hence, despite the high fees involved, a substantial investment in promotion and public relations, including advertising, is truly a wise use of resources. A company is only prepared to invest a small sum in promotion, the effect will be little or nothing at all. According to a Chinese proverb, this is like 'throwing a handful of salt into the sea to make it more salty'. Gift-giving or guest-treating for the purpose of enhancing relationships can also be a very expensive business in China.

The promotional cost of breaking into regional sales networks again can be very expensive. There are intangible expenses, such as the cost of establishing and maintaining business relationships. Businesses need to establish contact with the appropriate people at all levels of government and in the right networks. This is especially important if a product or service needs to have national exposure: breaking trade blockades between provinces, or between one large city and another. This is not only time-consuming, but also very costly. In a formal, Western accounting system this type of expense may not be counted as a legitimate business deduction against taxation. However, owing to the characteristics of Chinese business culture, any foreign company operating in China must be prepared to allocate capital resources to public relations, otherwise complete failure will ensure. The general manager or manager of a public relations department of a Chinese company is given a budget for building business relationships.

The Chinese government usually offers more favourable concessions to large companies that have strong financial backing, although it welcomes all foreign investment. Large companies with international reputations can easily catch the attention of the Chinese government at all levels. This leads to the dual advantages of financial protection and political support.

3. Predisposition: *Developing Relationships*

Previous chapters have demonstrated that China's social and economic systems are different from other countries and that China's business culture is unique. These conditions require that the interested foreign businessperson be fully briefed on all relevant government policies. It also suggests that foreign businesspeople establish sound commercial and interpersonal relationships at the beginning of any business venture in China.

Specific Industry Policies

Investing time in collecting and understanding information about Chinese's industrial and commerical policy is essential for new foreign investors in China. The Chinese government remains the predominant controller of the Chinese economy and its policies — a power that can limit or favour foreign investors. Failure to fully appreciate particular policies can lead to commercial disaster. Being fully conversant with current policy trends will minimise risk and identify supportive industry initiatives.

Knowing Business Partners

Investors in a joint venture in China need to first invest their time and energy into acquiring information about their potential partners. Ownership, financial power and the relative strengths and weaknesses of prospective Chinese partners must be determined in advance. In addition, the nature of a project must be comprehensively understood. Investors need to analyse relevant data to identify suitable partners for their business. As indicated in Chapter 5, there are three types of ownership in China, each with its own specific advantages and disadvantages in relation to obtaining governmental support. This includes financial back up, market orientation, and assistance programmes to increase industrial performance and the transfer and possession of technology.

A Chinese enterprise's motive in establishing a joint venture is either to acquire technological or managerial expertise or else to gain entry into an existing market for a particular product or financial resource. Whether or not a Chinese partner has sufficient financial strength to meet long term commitments as promised needs to be carefully determined in advance. A Chinese enterprise may possesses excellent technical staff or skilled workers, but may not have the financial capacity to complete the joint venture project on time or see it through to completion in the manner stipulated in the agreement. In the rush to attract foreign investment, some Chinese managers may fail to mention their own financial weaknesses. This may be out of a sense of embarrassment or it may be a deliberate ploy. Usually they will only inform their foreign partners about any difficult financial situation after both sides have invested substantial amounts of capital in the project. They will then force the foreign partners to put more and more capital in the project relying on the latter's desire not to lose their previous investment. Chinese businesspeople call this a 'fishing project', which means that they present their particular strengths and positive qualities as 'bait' to 'catch' a large investor. Although only a few Chinese enterprises use this tactic, foreign investors must avoid being trapped. Investigations prior to investment can easily avoid involvement in a fishing project.

Nurturing Guanxi

The most important preparation for doing business in China is to nurture a business network. Business failure is guaranteed without preparation in this field. Every enterprise in China must identify and establish a relationship with relevant Chinese officials, suppliers and other businesspeople. This matter can be likened to an insurance policy. Like all insurance policies, a premium must be paid before a risk is underwritten and an accident happens. The difference between ordinary paid-up insurance and 'network insurance' is that the former is quick and easy to procure. In contrast, it takes a long time to build up business relationships in China and a great deal of care to maintain them afterwards. The point is that these relationships are reciprocal — they should operate for mutual benefit. Chinese in both the business world and the bureaucratic system do not appreciate being approached for assistance only when it is convenient or useful to the supplicant. In such cases they feel that they are simply being made use of and they may subsequently be reluctant to offer their assistance again. An appropriate way is to be prepared for the relationship with the right people long before you conduct any real business with them. Chinese businesspeople accept this preparation as a long-term operation and believe that good business must nurture *guanxi* long before *guanxi* can be taken advantage of.

Document and Local Knowledge Preparation.

Due to the barriers of language and culture, a company's documents must be prepared in advance in both the English and Chinese languages. This will result in a streamlining of the negotiating process. This will in turn reduce the potential for misunderstandings to develop. A foreigner may easily find a Chinese national who has reasonable English language speaking skills but it is difficult to find a native Chinese speaker who is a qualified oral interpreter, fluent in writing as well as spoken English. It is even more difficult to find a qualified interpreter who is able to understand the subtleties of both Chinese and Western business cultures.

4. Personnel: *Recruiting the Right People*
There have been many concerns expressed about whether foreign investors should appoint local Chinese to senior positions within their China operations and whether a reduction in the number of expatriates and an increase in local staff is necessary. Further there has been a great deal of discussion about what kind of people should be chosen, if Chinese are to be chosen for managerial positions in joint ventures (Gamble, 2000; Li and Kleiner 2001). Throughout this book it has been argued that Chinese business culture is not only about professional know-ledge, technology, or the skills of business, but also involves many extra-commercial, sociological or cultural issues as well. A foreigner may master Chinese etiquette, language, political culture or economic policy by living in China for many years. However, he or she may still have difficulties in fully comprehending the psychology of the Chinese people and will continue to struggle with complex, culturally-based business matters. A foreigner can never understand the subtle cultural nuances and psychological traits of the Chinese people better than a native Chinese resident. Chinese businesspeople may treat foreign business partners as friends, sometimes overwhelmingly, but will

not accept them as Chinese who can understand their own subtle and complex business culture. Indeed, they tend to avoid being involved in business activities with these foreign 'friends' in the same way as with their compatriots. This creates many difficulties for foreign companies who wish to expand their business activities in China but regard putting local Chinese to important positions as an unjustified risk and rely solely on expatriates to run their business in China. Expatriates sometimes have 'natural authority' among Chinese employees because they respect the success of the foreign parent company in terms of technology, finance, or management skills. The development of international teams, including Chinese locals in senior positions, in foreign invested firms is suggested as an ideal way to expand business success in the long term.

At present, some offices or branches of large foreign companies have taken advantage of local knowledge by appointing Chinese nationals as senior managers or public relations managers. They have relied on them to effectively promote and develop company business in the Chinese market. A foreign executive manager has summarised this matter as "a businessperson needs people who know people, who can make decisions. In a country as diverse as China, without *guanxi*, without language skills, or local knowledge, a foreigner will never find the keys to the Celestial Kingdom's market place."

Finding skilled, experienced and trustworthy local people who are capable of exploring business opportunities and/or social relationships for the purpose of commerce is the key to success in China. This point should be considered carefully by new entrants to the market, especially those who intend to operate as wholly-owned foreign enterprises. These businesses have the disadvantage of not having Chinese partners who can provide the necessary local cultural knowledge or practical business experience to minimise risk. A successful foreign company in China must therefore be able to master the traits of Chinese business culture by either choosing the right local partner or else employing the right local person in an important position.

Case Study: Getting the Right Architect

KF Design Group is a national "A" class design joint venture between Western and Chinese partners, with headquarters located in Beijing. It has associate branches in Shanghai, Shenzhen, Dalian, Fuzhuo, Chengdu, Hong Kong and a number of other cities. Both sides are well-known and established architectural firms, with excellent reputations and track record. The Western partners, in particular, had designed many of their country's significant landmarks. They were members of the prestigious Royal Institute of British Architects and holders of a number of international awards. Based on international reputation, rich experience and an outstanding record, the Western partner confidently proposed to assign one of their staff as General Manager in charge of business, including organising tenders for projects for the joint venture. This decision was agreed by the Chinese side without dispute and the Western side felt that this would reduce some investment risk. However, business life in China proved difficult for the assigned expatriate, even though he was hard-working and very experienced in his job before coming to China. Although extremely diligent, he failed win any tenders for the joint venture. Consequently the performance of the joint venture and the morale of Chinese employees, of whom were all professionals, was diminished. The Head-quarters of the joint venture had no choice but have the expatriate replaced. This time a Chinese architect was appointed as GM. The expatriate was made Chairman of the board of the joint venture in Beijing. The reason for giving the crucial position at a critical time to this Chinese architect was that he had worked in both Beijing local and State architecture design institutes. He not only possessed rich experiences in various design projects in China, but also had an extensive *guanxi* network with people in charge of allocating projects, whom he had indirectly or directly worked with before joining the current joint venture. The situation of the firm improved immediately. New significant projects were awarded the Great Wall Sheraton Hotel in Beijing (for Interior Design), including the Overseas Investment Centre and Aijian Plaza in Shanghai. The Chinese GM and the Western Chairman collaborated closely and effectively co-ordinated the relationship between each parent companies in the joint venture. Together both men led their firm to a very high level of performance and commercial success, through a pragmatic understanding of the prevalent business conditions facing the joint venture.

Within the context of Chinese business culture, both the local manager and the expatriate contributed different strengths in relation to gaining the local market and communicating with the parent companies. As the case study shows, mis-posting people not only costs a company business, but can also lead to frustration, and even psychological damage, to expatriates. Problems are inevitable if appointment decisions are made only on considerations of risk reduction.

The most appropriate person to explore business opportunities in China could be defined as someone who has experience in dealing with both the local bureaucracy and media, and who also has knowledge of the relevant professional field. In most instances, experience in dealing with cultural issues is more important than professional knowledge. In Chinese business culture, an employee in a key or senior position must not only know the traits of Chinese business culture but must also be able to deal confidently with any issue by drawing on his or her extensive practical experience.

Case Study: A Hapless 'Pioneer'

A foreign company failed to develop business in China because they appointed an unsuitable person. The company placed a recruitment advertisement in their home country seeking a native Chinese to develop their business in the Chinese market. The advertisement outlined a number of employment principles. These included holding a higher degree in a related specialist field, professional knowledge in a technical area and bilingual language competency. In return the company offered an attractive salary package.

A Chinese person who had worked overseas was appointed according to the terms and conditions set out in the advertisement. He was then sent to China to explore the market on behalf of this foreign-owned technology company. This person was indeed both knowledgeable and experienced in his field of expertise. However, this same person had no idea whatsoever about the current state of Chinese commerce and was not at all familiar with the important commercial centres of Beijing, Shanghai and Guangzhou, since he had been studying and working in laboratories overseas. Nor did this person have the practical experience to deal with Chinese officials or the necessary connections to establish professional relationships on behalf of his foreign company. As a result, one year later, no substantive progress had been made. The hapless employee could find no way of effectively contacting the relevant governmental officials or prominent businesspeople. The lesson is that foreign companies operating in China recruit employees who are fully versed in the main aspects of Chinese business culture, both formal and informal, technical and intuitive.

Employers must be flexible about training new employees. The average Chinese worker is very disciplined, hard-working and possess reasonable skills. However, at present these same workers may have an underdeveloped sense of efficiency and participation compared with workers in some developed countries. As outlined, cultural values such as the 'Iron Rice Bowl' of state-owned organisations still exert a powerful influence on Chinese workers. Problems associated with these values, such as a poor appreciation of quality control, can be overcome by initiating a comprehensive training programme to improve the performance and outlook of Chinese workers at the very beginning of a venture. This will use half the effort for twice the outcome. The alternative is to ineffectually respond to problems as they arise rather that real workplace reforms.

5. Protection: *Legal Security*

For many foreign companies, the biggest impediment to conducting successful business in China is illegal or corrupt practices. The legal system in China is still far from easy to work with, although in recent years many new laws and acts have been passed. Some Chinese businesspeople have no sense of the importance of the rule of law. They behave as if are above the law. Besides the usual problems that occur from time to time between labour and management anywhere in the world, troubles such as violating contracts, bribery, corruption, violations against trademark rights and embezzlement occur. This situation is expected to improve dramatically now that China has joined WTO. To protect the rights and interests of business in China, every foreign and Chinese businessperson needs to know how to handle a range of illegal commercial activities.

- Background checking. A newcomer should know everything possible about the Chinese company or agency that he or she is going to deal with. The background check should include the partner's ownership status, financial strength, previous business performance, and the nature of their usual business, as well as their motive for becoming involved in the collaborative project. Combining all these relevant pieces of information, it is possible to make an informed judgement about whether or not the collaboration should go ahead. In the case of SOEs, it is crucial to check who is administratively in charge of the business, that is, which level of government supervises negotiations and which governmental department and government officer will be responsible for joint ventures and projects after negotiations are complete. This could be helpful in solving any dispute that might occur in the future by appealing to the hierarchy.

- Relevant law-checking. Make sure that the full extent of protection is available under Chinese law and that the policy afforded to a particular project or trade item is applied fairly. This is especially important when dealing with suspicious partners of doubtful repute.

- Proper contract signing. Sign contracts with a partner or new employees *before* the beginning of formal business co-operation; include items in the written contract that cover rights and responsibilities — in both Chinese and English, in as much detail as possible. A process for settling disputes must also be worked out in advance and then written into the contract.

- Applying anti-corruption skills introduced in Chapter 6.
- Strive for private/informal solutions first. Solving a dispute through trust in an informal way should be considered before a legal action in a dispute situation. Taking a dispute, especially a small issue, to the courts should not be the first choice in China. Legal resources in China are limited. The legal process is usually very slow and is still in the process of improvement. The number of lawyers as a percentage of the total population in China is low compared with some developed countries. For example there are 800,000 lawyers in the United States (Fatehi, 1996), which means that on average, there is one lawyer per 337 people. The percentage of lawyers in China is far lower. In some Western countries, the court is seen as an effective way to solve disputes. However, unlike Americans or other Westerners who view legal action as the best way to both defend and attack, Chinese partners view legal action as the worst way to handle a commercial problem. In these circumstances they believe that the other side is no longer suitable to do business with and prefer to halt any further co-operation. As mentioned in Chapter 4, it is believed that both sides' 'face' is damaged in this process.
- Arbitration and legal action. If the informal solution does not work or disputes occur, arbitration should be the first choice. In China one should not expect that the courts can always solve a legal dispute effectively. Often a business situation will become bitter before a satisfactory judgement is reached, if one party of the dispute does not initiate the game of *guanxi*. In China, there are four types of organisation that offer foreign companies legal assistance. They are the Foreign Economic and Trade Arbitration Commission; the Commission for Discipline Inspection of the CCP (at both the central and local levels); and the Foreign

Trader's Association. In addition, there are qualified and competent attorneys in every regional area, although this resource is usually limited.

6. Perspective: *Cultural Sensitivity*

The basic rule for conducting successful business in China is to show sensitivity to the host country's culture and attempt to understand the cultural differences that exist there (Fatehi, 1996). Confucian social values have shaped all aspects of Chinese culture. In general, the Chinese way of communication, of linking friendship with social life, plus traditional Chinese concepts of time, hierarchy, self-image, 'face', sense of risk taking, ways of conflict resolution, and perceptions of relationships are very different from those of most Western countries. These cultural dimensions can help to predict and explain Chinese business behaviour, consumer psychology, and employee work attitudes and behaviour. The only way to be effective in China is neither to correct these different cultural features nor blame them, but to understand and adapt to them, and at best to compromise with them.

Chinese culture is recognised as being highly complex and contextual, with a wide variety of different rules, linguistic expressions, gestures, and relationship principles that can be applied in different situations (Scheider and Barsoux, 1997). This causes difficulties for many Western people who are generally accustomed to a low context culture, which practices rules of direct communication universally, without considering contingent situations. One of most influential cultural dimensions of China is hierarchy. For Chinese people, the rules and ways of communication must be applied differently at different hierarchical levels. Conversely even though a great many cultural differences may exist between Western countries no matter how senior a position you hold or how senior in age you are, I may treat you more or less the same as anyone else in business matters. In contrast, in a Chinese context, a Chinese person would use a 'court expression', special title, humble gesture, specially arranged seating, and better-quality gifts to show respect for the seniors. He or she would also believe that regulations and laws apply less to seniors than to other people. In return, by being members of the senior's network, he or she would gain privileges and protection for their business activities.

It would be very unfortunate if someone wanting to do business in China unconsciously or consciously took their own cultural assumptions and moral standards as international ones and tried to impose them on their operations in China. It is better to use cultural analysis as a tool for doing business in China. This principle has been evoked throughout the whole book — by maintaining cultural sensitivity and applying cultural analyses to Chinese business operations, risk is reduced.

Making things more complicated is the fact that China, an immature market with many defects, is growing at a phenomenal rate. The political and cultural changes that took over two hundred years to unfold in the West and which have resulted in a distinctive Western and now international business culture, have been all but achieved in China in one generation. Traditional Chinese cultural values both clash and mix with Western cultures. This may inevitably result in changes to Chinese business values and behaviour. China's entry into the WTO will certainly accelerate this process. The astute businessperson can use the six 'P's, including cultural perspective, to evaluate the incalculable business potential of the PRC. They can then culturally, financially and technically prepare themselves for successful commerce and trade with the 'world's largest market'.

References

Adler, N. J. 1997 *International Dimensions of Organizational Behavior* (3rd edition). Ohio: South-Western College Publishing.

Alexander, C. N. and Knight, G. W. 1971 "Situated identifies and social psychological experimentation". *Sociometry*, 34, 65-82.

Arkin R. M. and Sheppard, J. A. 1989 "Self-presentation styles in organizations", in R.A. Giacalone and P. Rosenfeld, op.cit., 125-139.

Anonymous, 2000 Little Spenders, *Business China*, October 9

Anonymous, 2001 *China Information Daily*, June

Black J. S. 1988 Work Role Transitions: A Study of American Expatriate Managers in Japan, *Journal of International Business Studies*, Vol. 19; 277-294

Cheung, G. W. and Chow, I. H.S. 1999 Subcultures in Greater China: A comparison of managerial values in the People's Republic of China, Hong Kong and Taiwan, *Asia Pacific Journal of Management* 16 (3): 369-387.

China State Statistics Bureau, 2001.

Child, J. 1995 *Management in China during the age of reform*. Australia: Cambridge University Press.

Child, J. and Lu, Y. 1996 *Management Issues in China: Volume II International Enterprises*, London: Routledge.

Connor, N. and Chalos, P. 1999 The Challenge for Successful Joint Venture Management In China: Lessons From a Failed Joint Venture.' *Multinational Business Review* 7 (1): 50-61.

Cui, Geng and Liu, Oiming 2001 Executive insights: Emerging market segments in a transitional economy: A study of urban consumers in China, *Journal of International Marketing*, 9 (1): 84-99.

Fatehi, K, 1996 *International Management: A cross-cultural and functional perspective*. New Jersey: Prentice Hall.

Fang, T. 1999 *Chinese Business Negotiation Style*. London: SAGE Publications.

Feng, T. and Yen, H. T. 2001 'A concern with a gap of commonwealth incomes.' *Reader No 1:42-43.*

Feng, Y. L. 1985 *The History of Chinese Philosophy* (translation edition). Hebei: Beijing University Press.

Gamble, J., 2000 Localizing Management in foreign-invested enterprises in China: Practical, Cultural, and Strategic Perspective, *International Journal of Human Resource Management*, 11 (5): 883-903.

Glasser, P. and Pastore, R. 1998 West meets east. *CIO* 11 (1): 32-36.

Hoon-Halbauer, S. K., 1999 'Managing relationships within Sino-foreign joint ventures.' *Journal of World Business* 34 (4): 344-371.

Goffman, E. 1955 "On face-work: An analysis of ritual elements in social interaction". *Psychiatry*, 18 (3) 1955, 213-31, August. Republished in Erving Goffman (1972) *Interaction Ritual*, Penguin, 5-45.

Goodall, K., & Willem, B. 1998 Frequent fliers. *China Business Review*, 25(3): 50-53.

Goodfellow, R. O'Neill, D. and Smith, P. 1999 *Saving Face, Losing Face, In Your Face: A Journey into the Western Heart Mind and Soul*, , London: Butterworth Heinemann.

Hofstede, Geert 1980 *Culture's Consequences: International Differences in Work-Related Values*. Beverly Hills, CA: Sage

Hu, A. G. 2001 *Report of China economy*. Xinhu News Agency.

Kaye, M. and Taylor, W. G. K. 1997, Expatriate Culture Shock in China: A Study in the Beijing Hotel Industry, *Journal of Managerial*

Psychology, Vol. 12, No.8: 496-510.

Kluckhorn, F and Strodtbeck, F. L. 1961 *Variations in Values Orientation.* Illinois: Row Petersen

Lai, G. Y. and Ye, Q. 1999 *WTO: China's entry.* Xiamen: Xiamen University Press.

Lamb, C.W. Jr., Hair J. F. Jr. and McDaniel, C. 1996 *Marketing.* Ohio: South-Western College Publishing

Lau, C.M., Ngo, H. Y. and Chow, C. K. 1999 'Private businesses in China,' in Kelley, L. and Y. Pp. 25-48 in Kelley, L. and Luo, Y. (eds). *China 2000: Emerging Business Issues.* , London: Sage Publications.

Li, L. and B. H. Kleiner (2001), Expatriate-Local Relationship and Organisational Effectiveness: A Study of Multinational Companies in China *Management Research News*, 24, 3/4, pp 49-56.

Lian, J, 2001 China economy. Xinyua Agency.

Luo, Y. and M. Chen 1997 Does *Guanxi* Influence Firm Performance, *Asia Pacific Journal of Management,* 14, pp 1-16.

Martinsons, M. G. and Tseng, C. 1999 Technology transfer to China: Environmental considerations and emerging management practices, in Kelley, L. and Y. Luo, *China 2000.* London: SAGE Publications.

Park, H. S. and Luo Y. 2001 'Guanxi and organizational dynamics: Organizational networking in Chinese firms.' *Strategic Management Journal* 22: 455-477.

Parkhe, A., 1998 Understanding Trust in International Alliances *Journal of World Business,* 33 (3):219-240

Pascale, R. T. and Athos, A. G. 1981 *The Art of Japanese Management.* New York: Simon and Schuster.

Pearce, J. A. II and Robinsion, R. Jr. 2000 Cultivating *guanxi* as a foreign Investor strategy *Business Horizons* January-February.

Peill-Schoeller, P. 1994 Interkulturelles Management: Synergien in Joint Ventures zwischen China und deutschsprachien Landern, Spriger-

Verlag Berlin: Heridelberg

Robbins, S. P., Waters-Marsh, T., Cecioppe, R. and Millett, B. 1994 *Organisational Behaviour: concepts, controversies and applications.* Sydney: Prentice Hall.

Schneider, S. C and Barsoux J. L. 1997 *Managing across cultures.* London: Prentice Hall.

Steidlmeier, P, 1999 'Gift giving, bribery and corruption: Ethical management of business relationships in China.' *Journal of Business Ethics* 20 (2): 121-132.

Slater, Joanna
a. 1999 'Wrong Answer.' *Far Eastern Economic Review* 162 (43): 66-68.
b. 1999 'Sales force.' *Far Eastern Economic Review* 162 No. 13: 42-44

Standifird, S. S. and Marshall, R. S. 2000 'The transaction cost advantage of guanxi-based business practices, *Journal of World Business* 35 (1): 21-42.

Sun, L. 2000 Anticipatory ownership reform driven by competition: China's township- village and private enterprises in the 1990s, Comparative Economic Studies, 42(3): 49-47.

Tsang, Eric W.K. 1998 Can guanxi be a source of sustained competitive advantaged for doing business in China *Academy of Management Executive* 12 (2): 64 -73.

Walsh, J. P., Wang E. P and Xin, K R. 1999 Same bed, different dreams: Working relationship in Sino-American joint venture, *Journal of World Business* 34 (1): 69-93.

Wang, C. L., Chen, Z. X. and Chan, A. K. K. 2000 In influence of hedonic values on consumer behaviors: An empirical investigation, *Journal of Global Marketing*, 14 (1) (2): 169-186.

Wang, K.Y, and Clegg, S. 2002 Trust and decision making: Are managers different in the People's Republic of China and in Australia?, *International Journal of Cross-Cultural Management* 9 (1): 30-45.

Wang, Y. and Zhang, X. S. 1989 *Cultural Superiority: The Best Choice to Win Dominance in Competition.* Beijing: Xinwua Press

Wang, Y., Zhang, X. S. and Goodfellow, R. 1998 *Business Culture in China,* Singapore: Butterworth-Heinemann Asia-Reed Academic Publishing.

Worm, V. and Frankenstein, J., 2000, The Dilemma of Managerial Cooperation in Sino-Western Business Operations, *Thunderbird International Business Review,*. 42 (3): 261-238.

Wong, Y. H. and Chan, R. Y. 1999 'Relationship market in China: Guanxi, favoritism and adaptation.' *Journal of Business Ethics* 22 (2): 107-118.

Whelan, C. 2000 Emerging Market that Lives Up to Name, *Fortune* 142 (14): 184-188

Yan, A., 1999 International joint ventures in China: Interpartner characteristics, dynamics, opportunities and challenges for the new century, in Kelley, L. and Y. Luo, *China 2000,* pp. 25-48 *London*: SAGE Publications:

Yau, Oliver H. M., Lee, Jenny S. Y., Chow, Raymond P. M., Sin, Leo Y. M. and Tse, Alan C. B. 2000 'Relationship Marking the Chinese Way.' *Business Horizons* January-February.

Xin, F. 1995 'The Chinese cultural system: Implications for cross-cultural management.' *Sam Advanced Management Journal* 60 (1): 14-20.

Xue, Q.Z. 2000 *Multinationals and the Chinese Market.* Shanghai: Shanghai Press.

Zikmund, W. G. and D' amico, M. 1996 *Marketing,* New York: West Publishing Company.

Zhu, R. J. 2001 The annual report of the central government, the People's Republic of China.

About the Authors

Dr **Yuan Wang** (Ph.D. Management) is a consultant who specialises in Chinese business culture and international management combine with extensive knowledge of China's organisational culture, management and market. Dr Wang has consulted to private corporations and governmental organizations in both China and Australia. She has conducted research on international management and joint venture projects in both Chinese and international cultural settings.

Currently Dr Wang bases her academic work at The University of Technology Sydney, NSW, Australia, where she lectures at postgraduate (MBA) level. Dr Wang also holds a Professorship in the Faculty of Business, at The Renmin University of China.

Associate Professor Xin Sheng Zhang is an independent cross-cultural consultant and trainer. For many years Associate Professor Zhang was a senior educator in the Faculty of Adult Education, at The People's University of China, Beijing. Associate Professor Zhang has conducted extensive research on corporate culture in the People's Republic of China as a member of the research team of The Research Institute - Economic and Management System Reform, of The State Commission for Restructuring the (PRC) Economic System.

Associate Professor Zhang was one of the first scholars in The People's Republic of China to research and apply the theory of 'Public Relations' to both the Chinese academic and corporate fields.

Professor Zhang has published over ten books and many articles in the field of Chinese corporate culture, cross-cultural management and public relations. His expertise is in marketing communication and promotion in China. And has acted as an expert consultant for many multinational companies in both China and Australia since 1987. Currently, Associate Professor Zhang is a director of Australia-

China Economic Development Centre and a senior research fellow of the China Corporate Culture Association. (Contact details: *michaell957@sina.com.cn*).

Dr Rob Goodfellow (Ph.D. History) is an Australian-based author, journalist, researcher and cultural consultant who has extensive experience in the field of Chinese and Indonesian business and political cultures.

Dr Goodfellow's Master's of International Business course, 'Bridgehead Asia: Australian Business in the third millenium with special reference to Indonesia and the People's Republic of China,' and his recent publication on the topic, *Investing in Australia*, forms the basis of a highly successful onshore consultancy that briefs foreign trade delegations on Australian business protocol, culture, and social development.

Dr Goodfellow's specific consultancy expertise is in the field of identifying and managing cultural risk associated with cross cultural business exchange - through high level corporate briefings, advocacy, protocol training and the planning and implementation of appropriate strategies that minimise risk associated with misunderstandings based on different cultural perceptions. (Contact details: *sujoko@ozemail.com.au*).

Index

A

B

good luck, 54, 55

guanxi, 39, 47–51, 57, 91, 101, 110, 127, 130, 141-146, 148-154, 166, 170, 175, 195, 241, 249, 251, 253

gift-giving, 151, 152, 153, 154, 169, 170, 171, 172, 246

gifts, 150, 152, 153, 154, 155, 156, 169, 172

'grey income', 184

group solidarity, 24

gunboat diplomacy, 7, 8

H

head-hunting, 121

Heaven, 30, 32

hierarchical values, 48

high uncertainty avoidance, 47

Hong Kong, 4, 7, 9, 11, 12, 13

Hong Kong Special Administrative Region, 55

Huiecong International, 204, 205

hierarchy, 19, 20, 21, 22, 23, 24, 26, 28, 29, 32, 34

hierarchical values, 59, 61, 62

hospitality, 59, 80, 83, 87, 88

Huicong Group, 12

I

International Olympic Committee, xvi

iron rice bowl', xv, 41, 120, 255

inebriation, acceptability of, 82

informal non-business discussions, 65

interpreters, 63, 82

inter-departmental conflicts, 167

N

O

P